MEMORY
A Guide for Professionals

Alan J. Parkin

University of Sussex

JOHN WILEY & SONS, LTD

Chichester · New York · Weinheim · Brisbane · Singapore · Toronto

Copyright © 1999 by John Wiley & Sons Ltd,
Baffins Lane, Chichester,
West Sussex PO19 1UD, England

National   01243 779777
International   (+44) 1243 779777
e-mail (for orders and customer service enquiries):
cs-books@wiley.co.uk
Visit our Home Page on http://www.wiley.co.uk
or http://www.wiley.com

Other Wiley Editorial Offices

John Wiley & Sons, Inc., 605 Third Avenue,
New York, NY 10158-0012, USA

WILEY-VCH Verlag GmbH, Pappelallee 3,
D-69469 Weinheim, Germany

Jacaranda Wiley Ltd, 33 Park Road, Milton,
Queensland 4064, Australia

John Wiley & Sons (Asia) Pte Ltd, 2 Clementi Loop #02-01,
Jin Xing Distripark, Singapore 129809

John Wiley & Sons (Canada) Ltd, 22 Worcester Road,
Rexdale, Ontario M9W 1L1, Canada

Library of Congress Cataloging-in-Publication Data

Parkin, Alan J.
  Memory, a guide for professionals / Alan J. Parkin.
     p.   cm.
  Includes bibliographical references and index.
  ISBN 0-471-98302-0 (pbk.)
  1. Memory.   I. Title.

  BF371 .P275 1999
  153.1'2 21—dc21   99–045636

British Library Cataloguing in Publication Data

A catalogue record for this book is available from the British Library

ISBN 0-471-98302-0

Typeset in 11/13pt Palatino by Dorwyn Ltd, Rowlands Castle, Hants
Printed and bound in Great Britain by Biddles Ltd, Guildford and King's Lynn
This book is printed on acid-free paper responsibly manufactured from sustainable
forestry, in which at least two trees are planted for each one used for paper production.

MEMORY

Publishers' note

As this book goes to press, the Publishers have learned the sad news of Alan Parkin's death. We hope this book will be seen as a worthy part of Alan's substantial contribution to the field of memory studies, and as a legacy to his colleagues and to students of psychology.

All of us at John Wiley & Sons extend our deepest sympathies to Alan's family and friends, especially to his partner Frances and their daughter Verity.

CONTENTS

ABOUT THE AUTHOR

Alan Parkin is Professor of Experimental Psychology at the University of Sussex. He is an internationally recognised expert on human memory and its disorders, and the author of four recent books, *Memory and Amnesia* (2nd edn); *Memory: Phenomena, Experiment, and Theory*; *Explorations in Cognitive Neuropsychology*; *Neuropsychology of the Amnesic Syndrome*; and an edited volume *Case Studies in the Neuropsychology of Memory*. He has also published an extensive number of papers on memory and amnesia. In addition, he has appeared regularly on national radio and TV talking about memory and its disorders.

PREFACE

The aim of this book is to fill what I hope is an important gap in the range of books available about human memory. On the one side there are numerous textbooks about memory aimed directly at the academic market. On the other side there are books aimed directly at the general population. In my work as both an academic and a professional psychologist I have increasingly realised that there is a demand for a book that strikes the middle ground; one that is aimed at the professional who needs to know more about memory than the pop book provides but feels daunted by an academic text. What I have attempted here is an overview of human memory and, importantly, its pathology, that provides the essential facts about the issues that typically concern professionals such as lawyers, psychotherapists, psychiatrists, social workers and so on. The book will also be of value to those with a psychology background founded more in the humanistic domain of the subject. The account I provide is, I hope, relatively succinct but the interested reader will be able to pursue specific issues in detail by following up the notes and references at the end of each chapter.

1

MEMORY:
THE BASIC FACTS

Most of you reading this book are, presumably, largely un-familiar with the scientific investigation of memory. The aim of this first chapter, therefore, is to provide you with a basic map of how psychologists conceive of memory. This map can be thought of operating at two levels: the **psychological** and the **anatomical**. In the psychological section I consider ideas about memory that are not tied to the anatomy of the brain but instead consider memory in more abstract terms. The psychological ap-proach is not new: there are examples of this approach going back to the ancient Greeks. In contrast the anatomical approach provides you with information about which parts of the brain are concerned with memory. This is an area of research that has developed a great deal in the last twenty years or so.

THE PSYCHOLOGY OF MEMORY

When people complain about their memory they often claim that "my short-term memory is terrible", meaning that they frequently forget things that have happened to them in last few minutes, hours, days, or even months. Statements of this kind are, however, misleading because they imply that a single form of memory is responsible for remembering over all time periods. Research has now shown that there are two fundamentally dif-ferent forms of memory, which have very different characteris-tics, and are known as **short-** and **long-term store** (STS/LTS).

The idea of STS and LTS goes back to one of the first psycho-logists to write about memory, William James,[1] who made the astute observation that conscious mental activity required a form of memory. Understanding this sentence, for example, is only possible because you can hold "in mind" the first part while dealing with the second part. James described the form of memory, which we might think of as our span of awareness, as **primary memory** which he distinguished from a permanent store of knowledge called **secondary memory**. For James pri-mary memory represented the "rearward portion of the present space of time", information lingering in consciousness, which could be retrieved without effort. In contrast, information in secondary memory required effort to retrieve it because it had become part of the genuine past.

James's ideas about memory went largely unnoticed during the first half of the 20th century but were reconsidered around 1960 when psychologists once again became interested in the relationships between memory and conscious mental activity. Many experiments were set up to try to demonstrate the distinction between STS and LTS. One study made use of the "probe-digit" technique. Subjects monitored a stream of individually presented numbers (e.g. 1754982531) and, at various intervals a probe digit was presented (e.g. 2) and subjects had to say which number in the sequence had occurred immediately before it (8). The neat aspect of this experiment is that you can vary the number of digits between the target (7) and the probe digit (2)—in the current example there are four digits. It was found that subjects performed the task very easily when the number of intervening digits was four or less but that performance declined markedly when a higher number of digits occurred between target and probe.

Psychologists were quick to argue that the high level of performance achieved with four or fewer digits between target and probe arose because both were still in primary memory and thus consciously available whereas, with greater intervals, effortful retrieval from secondary memory was required and thus performance poorer. Other studies yielded similar conclusions. A common finding, for example, was that subjects showed very good recall of the last few words in a list they had seen or heard—a finding known as the **recency effect**—and attributed this effect to the last few words being in primary memory (see Figure 1.1).

SHORT- AND LONG-TERM STORE

If you open up the bonnet of your car you can, providing you have the appropriate mechanical knowledge, understand how

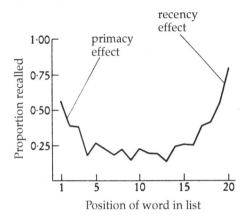

Figure 1.1: Typical results of a "free recall" experiment: Subjects are shown a list of words individually and, following the last one, are told to recall the words in any order they like. You can see that recall is highest for the last few words in the list and this is known as the "recency" effect. The recency effect is thought to reflect the output of STS. Recall from earlier parts of the list is lower and assumed to be the product of LTS. There is some advantage for the first few words of the list and this is known as the "primacy" effect. The primacy effect arises because subjects are able to pay more attention to these items during learning and there is also less interference from other words they are trying to remember. (From Glanzer, M. & Cunitz, A.R. (1966) Two storage mechanisms in free recall. *Journal of Verbal Learning and Verbal Behaviour*, **5**, 351–360).

the various components of the engine interact in order for the car to move. Unfortunately the same cannot be said of the brain. Thus when we examine the brain we can see its various parts but this does not help us to understand how it achieves its various functions, including memory—there is, as yet, no brain mechanic. As a result, psychologists are forced to use analogies as the basis for explaining how the brain carries out particular tasks—that is, a particular brain function is conceived of in terms of something we do understand. The 1960s witnessed the rapid development of computers and it did not take psychologists long to draw an analogy between the operation of computers and the mechanisms of human memory. As a result

James's distinction between primary and secondary memory was replaced with the concept of **short-** and **long-term store** (**STS** and **LTS**). Short-term store was seen as analogous to the central processing unit of a computer and secondary memory corresponded to the database. New information was inputted to STS and then, if required, transferred to LTS for storage. At a later point the information could then be restored to STS by **retrieval**.[2]

STS and LTS are, like all other brain activity, the products of biological processes. This being so it should be possible to find biological evidence supporting the distinction we have drawn between these two types of memory. The basic component of the brain is the nerve cell or **neurone**. There are many millions of these and they connect with one another by junctions known as **synapses**. The transmission of a nerve impulse across a synapse involves the production of a chemical known as a **neurotransmitter**. One of the most well-known neurotransmitters is **acetylcholine** and it is well established that memory will not function efficiently if insufficient amounts of this chemical are available—many of you will be familiar with the devastating effects that Alzheimer's disease has on memory and it is thus no surprise to learn that people with this disease have a marked lack of acetylcholine.

While Alzheimer's disease represents a permanent loss of acetylcholine it is also possible to temporarily inhibit the activity of this neurotransmitter with certain drugs. The most common of these drugs is **scopolamine**—a common constituent of travel sickness pills—and many studies have examined how the administration of this drug affects human memory. In one study[3] subjects were required to carry out three simple memory tasks. The first of these is **digit span** which involves the presentation of a short series of digits (e.g. 2, 7, 8, 1, 5) followed by the instruction to recall them immediately in the correct order. The task is graded, beginning with short sequences which increase in size until the subject is no longer accurate. This task has been used for many years and it has been established that a typical adult has a span of 7 plus or minus 2 a value which is thought to indicate the limitations of STS capacity. The second task was

supraspan in which the subject was asked to recall lists of digits larger than the known capacity of digit span (e.g. 10 digits) thus placing demands on both STS and LTS. Finally there was a test loading predominantly on LTS in which subjects saw a list of words and were asked to recall them later.

The results of the experiment were very clear. Administration of scopolamine had no effect on digit span, a small effect on supraspan, but resulted in a substantial impairment of free recall. Thus, along with the psychological evidence we have discussed, this experiment provides biological evidence for the STS/LTS distinction in that administration of the drug appears to have prevented transfer of information from STS to LTS. This process of transfer is known as **consolidation** and although our knowledge of how it occurs is far from complete it seems certain that the formation of new memories involves permanent changes in the synaptic connections between neurones. Other drugs, notably alcohol, benzodiazepines, and marijuana, can also disrupt consolidation, as can a sudden shock or interruption.

THE ORGANISATION OF LONG-TERM STORE

So far we have concluded that human memory essentially comprises two stores: short- and long-term store. However, there is a lot more to the organisation of memory than that. In particular it is clear that long-term memory is not a large amorphous store containing all the knowledge we have acquired. Rather, it is often thought to have three components: **procedural**, **semantic** and **episodic memory**[4].

The easiest distinction to accept is that between procedural memory on the one hand and semantic and episodic on the other. Most people reading this book will have one skill or more, such as typing or playing a musical instrument. Take a moment to reflect on what you can consciously recall about these skills (e.g. how are my fingers manipulated to type Brighton, or where do my fingers go to play the chord of A?) and you will notice that not much comes to mind. Instead you will be forced to perform the skills and get the information by observing your own pattern of movements. This is because the memory systems underlying these skills are procedural in nature—that is, they are represented in a way that is not consciously accessible. Some skills may initially rely on conscious knowledge for their acquisition (e.g. remembering finger positions on a keyboard) but become purely procedural with practice. Others, such as riding a bicycle, are procedural from the outset because the knowledge being acquired cannot be described verbally.

The distinction between semantic and episodic memory relates to the difference between knowledge about the world and memory for personal events. Thus a test of semantic memory would be a question such as "What is the capital of Peru?" whereas a test of episodic memory might be the question "What did you watch on television last night?". In the laboratory, measurement of these forms of memory involves particular types of memory test. Semantic memory might be assessed by using a verification task in which a person has to decide whether a statement is true or false (e.g. Can a penguin fly?). In contrast, episodic memory would be tested by giving the person a list of words to learn and asking him or her to recall them at a later point.

The above seems to be quite simple but, in reality, it is much more difficult to distinguish semantic and episodic memory clearly. One particular problem is that people may often use semantic memory as a basis for answering a question that appears to address episodic memory. Thus, if someone asks you what school you went to the answer you provide may be based on general knowledge about yourself (e.g. I know I went to Battersea Grammar School) as opposed to any specific personal recollection of your school days. Conversely, episodic memory can sometimes be used to answer questions that appear to rely on semantic memory. Thus, if asked a question such as "What is the quickest way to Brighton?" you might recall a previous time you had given that information and use that as the basis for answering.

Although the terms "semantic" and "episodic" are widely used it can be seen that they lack a certain precision in that psychologists have found it hard to show that they represent separate systems. This has led to the use of an umbrella term, **declarative memory**[5], as an alternative way of describing these forms of memory. The term "declarative" simply means access- ible to consciousness and thus provides a perfect contrast with procedural memory which, as we saw, defines memories that cannot be consciously described. Ideas about the organisation of LTS are summarised in Figure 1.2.

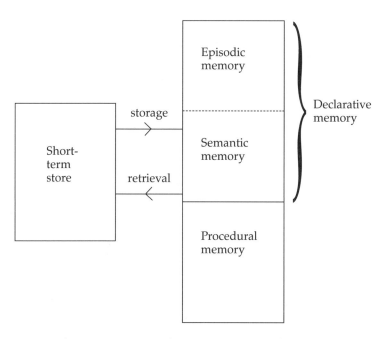

Figure 1.2: The organisation of memory. STS is the memory system supporting conscious mental activity. It interacts with the LTS—the permanent store by passing new information in and by retrieval. LTS is thought by some to have three components but others argue that the episodic and semantic systems should be lumped together as "declara- tive memory".

MEMORY AND THE BRAIN

Between the 1930s and 1950s neurosurgeons made widespread use of a procedure known as **temporal lobectomy** as a means of treating epileptic seizures that could not be controlled by drugs. The operations were successful in treating epilepsy but often had a very serious side effect in that the patients suffered **amnesia**—severe loss of memory (see Chapter 6). At the time the surgeons believed that the critical structure they had damaged in the operations was the **hippocampus**—so-called because of its resemblance to a seahorse (see Figure 1.3). However, it was not until 30 years later that this was confirmed in the study of a man who suffered a small stroke which caused damage only within the hippocampus. Investigations showed that this man had great problems remembering new information—a condition psychologists call **anterograde amnesia**—but, intriguingly he showed virtually no **retrograde amnesia**—problems in remembering information acquired prior to his brain injury.[6]

These initial findings have now been shown in another patient and confirm that the hippocampus appears essential for the consolidation of new memories. However, because most patients with temporal lobe damage, either lobectomy or other causes (see Chapter 5) have both anterograde and retrograde amnesia, it follows that other parts of the temporal lobe must be involved in the storage of memories. There is now considerable evidence that areas of the temporal lobe known as the **neocortex** appear to be the storage areas because damage to these areas produces profound retrograde amnesia.

Up until recently it was thought that consolidation was a rapid process but further investigations have suggested that this might not be the case. A number of patients have been reported who have damage to the hippocampus and adjacent structures such as the **subiculum** and the **dentate gyrus**, which go together to make up the hippocampal formation. As one would expect, these patients exhibited anterograde amnesia but they also had a severe retrograde amnesia extending back as much as 25 years.

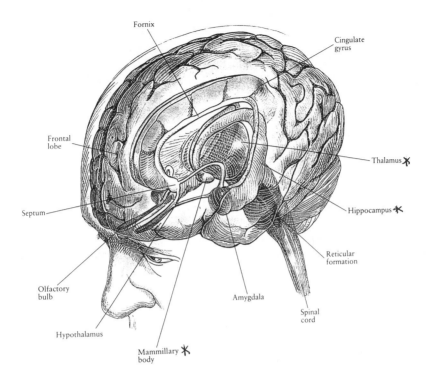

Figure 1.3: The human brain revealed. Structures labelled with an asterisk are known to be involved in memory in that when they are damaged they can give rise to a profound amnesia. Two other structures are also worthy of comment. The fornix is a large pathway that runs from the hippocampal formation to the mamillary bodies and it has been claimed that this can produce an amnesia as dense as damage to the structures it connects (Gaffan, D. & Gaffan, E.A. (1991) Amnesia in man following transection of the fornix. *Brain*, **114**, 2611–2618) but others suggest a milder deficit. The amygdala, which lies adjacent to the hippocampus, is specifically concerned with emotion, and damage here results in a person who is unable to remember the emotional aspects of events (Adolphs, R. et al. (1997) Impaired declarative memory for emotional material following bilateral amygdala damage. *Learning and Memory*, **4**, 291–300). (Adapted from Bloom, F.E. & Lazerson, A. (1988) *Brain, Mind and Behavior* (2nd edn). New York: Freeman. Reprinted with permission.)

These structures are considered far too small to be storage sites and the only conclusion is that they are involved in the consolidation of memories in the neocortex—thus even when the neocortex is unaffected damage to these adjacent structures will lead to the disruption of memories. Furthermore, the fact that memories dating back as much as 25 years can be affected suggests that consolidation is an extremely long-term process.

The temporal lobes are not the only brain region involved in memory. It has been known for some time that a region of the brain known as the **diencephalon** is also crucial for memory. Some of our evidence for this comes from patients who have suffered bizarre accidents such as having a snooker cue rammed up their nose but, predominantly, the evidence comes from people who have developed Korsakoff's syndrome as a consequence of alcoholism. Heavy drinking can interfere with the ability to metabolise thiamine which, in turn, leads to bleeding in the diencephalic region. Sometimes the effects of this bleeding are reversible but very often it is not and the outcome is a person whose primary impairment is a severe loss of memory involving both anterograde and retrograde amnesia. Autopsies on Korsakoff patients show a reasonably consistent pattern of brain damage in that parts of the **thalamus** along with an area known as the **mamillary bodies** are consistently damaged (see Figure 1.3). From this we can infer that these structures are also crucially involved in memory in some way.[7]

Although we know that the diencephalic region is involved in memory, its exact role is not clear. One idea is that it is crucial for enabling **context** to be incorporated into memory. We will encounter a lot more about context in the next chapter but, for now, it is sufficient to know that context corresponds to the information we store away which enables memories to be distinguished from one another in time and place. Context thus enables us to remember which of two events came first and where a particular event might have happened.

Finally, there is a third region of the brain involved in memory—the **frontal lobes** (again see Figure 1.3). There has probably been more speculation about what the frontal lobes do than any other part of the brain. For a long time it has been known that the frontal lobes play an essential role in maintaining the integrity of our personality and that damage to this area can produce a person who is socially disinhibited.[8] More recently it has also been realised that the frontal lobes play an important role in human memory.[9]

SUMMARY

- Human memory can be understood at a psychological level and an anatomical level.
- Psychologically memory is conceived of as two stores: STS and LTS.
- LTS can be divided into three separable components: procedural, semantic and episodic memory.
- Procedural memories are not consciously accessible and correspond to abilities such as skills.
- Semantic and episodic memories are both consciously accessible. Semantic memory relates to general knowledge, episodic memory is a record of our personal experiences.
- Distinguishing semantic and episodic memory can be difficult and some people prefer the single term "declarative memory" to cover both.
- New memories are created by the process of consolidation which involves permanent changes in the synaptic connections between neurones.
- Areas of the temporal lobe, diencephalon, and frontal lobes are essential for memory.
- Within the temporal lobe the hippocampus is crucial for initial consolidation, whereas other structures are involved in the longer term establishment and storage of memories.

NOTES AND REFERENCES

1. James, W. *Principles of Psychology*, vol. 1. New York: Henry Holt.

2. Accounts of the STS/LTS theory can be found in many places including most "Introduction to Psychology" texts. Some recommendations are: Baddeley, A.D. (1997) *Human Memory: Theory and Practice*, chap. 3. Hove: Psychology Press. Eysenck, M.W. & Keane, M. (1995) *Cognitive Psychology: A Student's Handbook*, pp. 126–129. Hove: Psychology Press. Parkin, A.J. (1993) *Memory: Phenomena, Experiment and Theory*, chap. 1. Oxford: Blackwells.

3. Drachman, D.A. & Sahakian, B.J. (1979) Effects of cholinergic agents on human memory. In R. Barbeau et al. (eds) *Nutrition and the Brain*, vol. 5. New York: Raven Press.

4. This distinction was proposed by Endel Tulving and there are a number of accounts of the concepts. See: Tulving, E. (1983) *Elements of Episodic Memory*. Oxford: Oxford University Press. Tulving, E. (1985) How many memory systems are there? *American Psychologist*, **40**, 385–398. Tulving, E. (1989) Memory, performance, knowledge, and experience. *European Journal of Cognitive Psychology*, **1**, 3–26.

5. See Squire, L.R. (1987) *Memory and Brain*. Oxford: Oxford University Press.

6. See Parkin, A.J. (1997) Memory: hippocampus is the key. *Current Biology* **6**, 1583–1585.

7. For details of the neuroanatomy of memory see Parkin, A.J. & Leng, N.R.C. (1993) *Neuropsychology of the Amnesic Syndrome*. Hove: Erlbaum.

8. See Kolb, B. & Whishaw, I.Q. *Fundamentals of Human Neuropsychology* (4th edn), chap. 14. New York: Freeman.

9. A recent account of frontal lobe function and memory is given by Parkin, A.J. (1997) *Memory & Amnesia: An Introduction* (2nd edn), chap. 7.

2

MECHANISMS OF MEMORY

All stimulation generates a memory—and these memories have to go somewhere. Our bodies are essentially diskettes.

(Douglas Coupland)

The selective memory isn't selective enough.

(Blake Morrison)

In this chapter we will be concerned with two crucial aspects of memory: remembering and forgetting. The first section will deal with the frequently cited idea that memory is essentially a passive process in which all experiences are faithfully recorded and where all forgetting is conceived of as a failure to remember. Having convinced you that memory is far better conceived of as a selective process in which most of what we experience is disregarded, I will then show how memory must be viewed as a reconstructive process rather than one in which the contents of memory are automatically retrieved. Next I will illustrate the central role that context plays in remembering and explore how psychoactive and emotional factors can influence how well we remember. Most of us assume that memory is inextricably linked with consciousness but I will describe recent work showing that we often remember information without being aware of it. Finally, I will consider the various ways in which forgetting occurs.

THE MYTH OF TOTAL RECALL

One of the most frequent misconceptions about memory is that all forgetting occurs as some form of retrieval failure—the idea being that, rather like a video recorder, every moment of our experience is faithfully recorded in memory and that forgetting occurs because we cannot access a particular memory. The pervasive nature of this mistaken view has many implications, not in the least providing false credibility to the idea that hypnosis can facilitate enhanced recall of forgotten experiences (see Chapter 7). However, a moment's thought indicates that a memory system that stored away everything would not be particularly likely or effective. Contrary to what some people claim, there is no part of the human brain that is unused and through the process of evolution different parts of the brain have evolved to do different things. Given that there is not an infinite capacity to expand the brain there has inevitably been pressure on space which, in turn, has meant that mental processes must be organised efficiently. From this perspective a memory system that stored everything away would be inefficient because of the large amount of space it would take up storing away information that we would never need. A far more effective memory system would be one that was **selective** in its operation in that only relevant aspects of experience were remembered.

It seems obvious that selectivity is the most sensible way to organise a memory system, so how did the video recorder notion of memory come about? The answer lies in experiments carried out by the neurosurgeon Wilder Penfield during the 1930s, 1940s and 1950s. In the last chapter we considered the procedure known as temporal lobectomy. A curious fact about these operations is that they are often carried out while the patient is conscious and this enables the surgeon to examine the effects of stimulating the brain's surface on the patient's conscious mental activity. During the operations Penfield frequently stimulated the brain of his patients and became intrigued by their responses. In particular he noted that stimulation of the temporal lobe caused the patients to spontaneously recall memories. This in itself is not surprising because, as we saw in the previous chapter, the temporal lobes are heavily implicated in memory. What impressed Penfield, however, was the apparent triviality of these memories. Thus the patients would recall events such as sitting on a wall looking at a Coca-Cola factory rather than major life events. Penfield believed that the trivial nature of these memories argued against any selective notion of memory and suggested instead that he had located the "stream of consciousness"—all memories are there but for some reason most become inaccessible.[1]

Penfield's idea had a lot of appeal and, as is so often the case in science, attractive ideas survive for a long time before anybody re-examines the evidence upon which they were based. In 1980 the psychologists Elizabeth and Geoffrey Loftus discovered that not only were Penfield's ideas popular with the public, they were also believed by a large number of professional psychologists.[2] This prompted them to look again at Penfield's evidence. The strength of Penfield's idea derived from the high frequency with which he had recorded memories during operations. Penfield conducted many operations and, according to his records, brain stimulation elicited recollections in a large number of them. However, when Loftus and Loftus reviewed the evidence they found only a handful of specific recollections with most "memories" being rather vague and, in many instances, clearly responses to the immediate circumstances.

MEMORY AS A SELECTIVE PROCESS

Memory, therefore, is not a passive all-embracing record of our lives. It is an actively selective system which stores away some aspects of our experience but discards others. Put another way, our total experience may reside initially in STS but only certain parts of that experience undergo consolidation and become part of LTS. The next question is: What determines the contents of LTS?

One of the key factors determining memory is the manner in which information is **encoded**. The idea of encoding is one you will be familiar with in other ways. When you use a telephone, for example, the sound waves of your voice are translated into an electrical current, transmitted down a cable, and then reprocessed to give a representation of your voice. In the same way memory works by encoding some features of an event, storing them in LTS, and then reprocessing them to give you a recollection of that event.

There is now plenty of evidence showing that the way we encode information can determine how well we remember it. A simple demonstration of this involves two groups of people each attempting to remember the same sequence of unrelated words. One group are asked to think about each word and decide whether or not it is pleasant while the other group count the number of syllables in each word. The results are clear cut: when asked to either recall the words or recognise them among a list in which the words are mixed in with words that were not presented, people who made the pleasantness judgement perform far better than those who just counted the syllables. The reason for this is that the two types of judgements have led subjects to select different features of the words when learning them. Pleasantness judgements cause people to encode the **meaning** of the words, whereas syllable counting does not.[3]

In the experiment we have just considered the participants were told to learn the material—so-called **intentional learning**. However, if we repeat the experiment without any instructions to remember, i.e. just ask subjects to make the same decisions but give them a surprise memory test, we get essentially the same result. The outcome of this **incidental learning** experiment thus suggests that intentionality is not the key to remembering. What is most important is the extent to which we process the meaning of what it is we are trying to learn.

The central role of meaning in memory goes some way towards explaining one of the most infuriating aspects of human memory. We can now understand why negative things so often stay in our minds whereas things we wish to remember do not. For something to be negative we clearly must understand it, its negativity impresses us, and it is this which imparts memorability. In contrast, if we are having difficulty understanding something then, no matter how hard we try, we will not remember it well. This last point is nicely illustrated in an experiment which compared the ability of novices and chess experts to remember the pattern of pieces on a chess board. The study showed that when patterns depicting stages in real games were used, the experts remembered far more than the novices. However, when improbable patterns were used there was no difference between the groups. This experiment shows that there was no absolute difference in the memory ability of the two groups. The experts only showed an advantage when they could use their knowledge of chess to impart greater meaning to the pattern of pieces.[4]

MEMORY AS A RECONSTRUCTIVE ACT

In the preceding section we saw that memory involves the selective storage of features via the process of encoding. The next step is to explain how, having stored memories away, we are able to access them via the process of **retrieval**. Once again the thoughts of William James are informative.

> *Suppose I am silent for a moment and then say . . . Remember!, Recollect! Does your . . . memory obey the order, and reproduce any definite image from your past? Certainly not. It stands staring into vacancy, and asking, What kind of a thing do you wish me to remember?*[5]

What James is emphasising here is that memory is a **reconstructive** act in which the act of remembering is triggered by some form of cue. To understand this, answer the question "What was the last meal you had in a restaurant?" "Well I must have begun with a starter, oh yes, it was mussels in a chilli sauce; next, main course, I remember, it was the beef fillet, dessert, I don't usually have one, so yes, just a cappuccino to finish." Here you can see how the initial cue about what tends to happen in a restaurant leads to the recollection of more specific memories.

As well as illustrating the basic reconstructive nature of memory the above example also introduces another important property of memory—its reliance on what have been termed **schema** (pl. **schemata**) or alternatively **scripts**.[6] A schema can be defined as a model of the world based on past experience which can be used as a basis for remembering events. Thus in the above example, general knowledge about what tends to happen in restaurants provides a framework within which to retrieve specific facts. From an economical point of view schemata are a good idea because they reduce the amount of information that an individual needs to store away. Thus, the same general schema about restaurants can be used when recovering information about different meals. Thus all that needs to be stored away about a particular meal are those aspects which differentiate it from other meals.

While one might consider schemata to be generally a good thing they do have disadvantages in that they can create distortions in memory. This was nicely illustrated by Frederick Bartlett, the British psychologist responsible for the concept of schemata. Bartlett conducted a series of studies exploring how undergraduates remembered a North American Indian folk story known as the "War of the Ghosts".[7] Here is an excerpt:

> *One night two young men from Egulac went down to the river to hunt seals and while they were there it became foggy and calm. Then they heard war-cries and they thought: "Maybe this is a war party." They escaped to the shore, and hid behind a log. Now canoes came up and they heard the noise of paddles, and saw one canoe coming up to them . . .*

After hearing the story initially the undergraduates returned to recall the story on several subsequent occasions. Bartlett noticed a number of systematic features of these subsequent recalls. First, there were frequent omissions, not only of details, but also aspects of the passage that were inconsistent with the undergraduates' own view of the world—many subjects, for example, frequently forgot the supernatural dimension of the story. The undergraduates also introduced rationalisations into the story and commonly substituted words used in the story with more familiar words. Thus "something black came out of his mouth" became "foaming at the mouth" and "canoes" became "boats".

Bartlett thus showed how people can use their own view of the world to distort what they actually heard. Bartlett's experiments were harmless in that the undergraduates were simply using their own knowledge to fill in gaps in their memory. However, schemata can have much more sinister effects on memory by introducing bias into people's recollections. A remarkable example of this came in the trial of the Watergate conspirators. A key witness for the prosecution was John Dean who, at the time, claimed he had a verbatim memory of all his conversations in the Oval Office. However, unknown to Dean, all these conversations had been taped and when compared with his account it was clear that Dean did not have a very good recollection at all. For example, Dean claimed that Nixon was impressed with his performance when this was not the case. It seems that Dean had constructed a schema about his role in the affair and distorted his recollections to fit with it.[8]

FORMS OF REMEMBERING

Up until now we have used rather general terms such as "remembering" to explain the operation of memory. However, it is now necessary to be a little more precise and define three basic forms of remembering:

- **Recall:** the person attempts to produce information from memory without any specific help—e.g. "tell me the words I showed you five minutes ago".
- **Cued recall:** the person is given specific cues to help recall, e.g. "one of the words I showed you five minutes ago began with A".
- **Recognition:** the person is given a list of words to look at and must indicate which of them were in the list he or she saw five minutes ago.

Recall and cued recall are both reconstructive in nature in that only partial information about the required memory is present. Recognition is, however, more complex. A common experience is to meet someone in the street and instantly become aware that you know the person but are totally unable to identify him or her. Psychologists call this initial form of recognition a **familiarity response** and it enables us to know that we have previously encountered that person. However, in order to fully recognise the person an additional form of memory must occur, **recollection**, in which the specific circumstances of that previous encounter are established. Recollection is effectively a form of cued recall because what we are doing is effectively using the cue provided by the person's face to reconstruct additional information about that person.[9]

CONTEXT

When we base a recognition response on just familiarity information we are effectively identifying someone in isolation—not relating it to anything else in our memories. However, when recollection occurs additional information about time and place of encounter is added to that initial response to provide a fuller memory of the individual that enables him or her to be distinguished from all other people we know. Psychologists use the term **context** to define this kind of information and the term **target** to define the memory with which the context is associated.

Unfortunately the term context is too broad and to gain a fuller understanding we must distinguish between two types of context, **intrinsic** and **extrinsic**. Intrinsic context describes information that bears directly on the identity of, for example, a person. Thus associations such as the person's hair colour, husband's name, and place of employment are essential parts of the context associated with the person's face. Our own experience tells us how essential intrinsic context is to remembering. All of you will, I am sure, have experienced recognition failure when you encounter a friend or acquaintance in an unusual setting (e.g. meeting a student on the beach in Turkey). This arises because the cues available to help reconstruct the context of that person are incompatible with those you have associated with that person. You maintain a feeling of familiarity but the context is hard to establish.

No one doubts that intrinsic context exerts a powerful influence on memory but there is less certainty about extrinsic context—which can be defined as features associated with a target which are not relevant to memory for the target. Thus a person at school may be attempting to learn the periodic table on a Tuesday morning in Classroom B which, on that day, was smelling of gloss paint because it had just been decorated. Here the periodic table serves as the target and factors surrounding that learning serve as **extrinsic context** (e.g. time, place, environmental characteristics).

Many experiments have explored whether extrinsic context is relevant to memory. More specifically, is it the case that presence of the same extrinsic context when trying to remember the target material will be an aid to recall because memory for the target material is somehow linked to the context? In the experiments, subjects study target material in a particular extrinsic context and are then required to try to remember the targets either in the same context used during learning or in a different context. One of the most well-known investigations of context involved divers learning word lists either on land or underwater. It was found that the divers remembered more when the environment at learning and test was the same than when, for example, they learned the list underwater and recalled it on dry land. Thus cues provided by the context appeared important in retrieving the target information.[10]

One can, of course, question the relevance of the diving study because few of us have to use our memories under such extremely different contexts. Indeed, it is a concern that the authors of the diving study felt the need to use extremes of contexts as the only means of guaranteeing an effect. However, a much more relevant setting is the classroom: Is it possible that target information learned in one room will be recalled better if testing also takes place in that room? Several studies have shown that information is recalled better when learning and test occur in the same room but there are two important reservations. First, the effects are small and, second, they can be overcome with a simple strategy—by instructing subjects to imagine their classroom immediately before test there is no benefit from being tested in the same classroom as that used in learning.[11]

So far we have thought of extrinsic context in terms of the external characteristics of the environment, but it is possible to extend the idea of context to include internal bodily states such as our emotional condition and any alterations to our consciousness caused by psychoactive substances such as alcohol or drugs. Applying the same experimental logic, is remembering easier when our psychoactive state is the same as that present during learning?

STATE-DEPENDENT LEARNING

Psychoactive drugs, both legal and illegal, are widely used in our society and there has been considerable interest as to whether the variations in internal states caused by these substances have implications for remembering: is it the case that if we learn target information in an intoxicated state we will remember it more effectively if we are in the same intoxicated state?—a phenomenon known as **state-dependent learning**. This area has been somewhat confused with many studies showing state-dependent effects and others not. There were various explanations for this, including the idea that only certain drugs would show the effect or that effects would only be obtained with higher levels of intoxication. Neither of these was correct. The explanation of variability lies in the type of test used. When studies which asked subjects to recall the information were examined, most of them showed state-dependent effects. However, studies employing cued recall or recognition typically failed to show state-dependent effects.[12]

Why should psychoactive states affect recall but not recognition? As we saw above recognition memory is a complex response in that something can be recognised in one of two ways—familiarity or recollection—with only the latter requiring any reconstructive retrieval activity. In contrast, recall necessarily involves reconstructive work. A study carried out on the effects of marijuana on memory asked subjects to indicate the associations they formed to words. It was found that associations formed under the influence of marijuana were different and less typical than those formed in a non-drugged state.[13] It is well established that associations made during learning form an important part of what is remembered about target information. Thus, at retrieval, the subject may well attempt to make contact with those associations as part of the reconstructive process. State-dependent effects on recall may therefore occur because, in the case of intoxication at learning and test, the subject is more likely to think of those atypical associations. In contrast we saw that recognition memory does not necessarily depend on recollective memory and that an effective response can be based on the non-reconstructive familiarity response. This may well be the reason why state-dependent effects are not found with recognition memory.

Before leaving this topic it is important to stress that studies examining state-dependent memory typically use drug doses that would not be considered excessive. Studies involving alcohol, for example, would use levels similar to the recommended safe limits. Excess levels of alcohol have a markedly different effect on memory, as many of you may well know! Hopefully few of you will have experienced blackouts or "lost weekends" but I expect many of you will have had difficulty remembering conversations you had when you were drinking quite a lot. Memories for these conversations would not return with similar levels of intoxication because the effects of alcohol at higher doses significantly disrupt memory consolidation. The same is also true of drugs such as marijuana.

EMOTION AND MEMORY

The possible effects of emotion on memory have a long history. One influential idea is that normal people have a bias towards recalling the more positive aspects of their experience—this has been variously termed the **hedonic selectivity theory** or the **Pollyanna effect**. The alternative theory is the **mood congruency theory** which argues that the mood someone is in during learning has a selective effect on encoding in that subjects will be biased to encoding those aspects of events which overlap with their mood state—happy people remember positive things, sad people remember negative things.[14]

Evidence for hedonic selectivity came largely from self-report studies where subjects were asked to recall events in their lives. Studies of this kind have a major flaw in that what subjects remember may be very different from what they say they remember. Thus a subject may have a very negative memory but, because of embarrassment, choose to recall a less important positive memory. The mood congruency theory has been investigated by more scientific methods although there are still some major methodological problems. The principal problem is that normal people do not show great variation in mood so that, within a sample of 100 people, only a handful would be either very elated or very sad. So, in order to investigate mood effects it is first necessary to make people happy or sad. This can be done in various ways such as exposing them to cheerful or depressing music, positive or negative statements about the future of the world, or via hypnosis-induced mood change.

Using these methods it has been shown that there appears to be some truth in the mood congruency effect. In one experiment subjects were hypnotically induced to feel happy or sad and then exposed to words with either strong negative (e.g. ulcer) or positive (e.g. beauty) connotations. The next day, free of any induced mood, subjects were asked to recall as many words as possible: previously sad subjects recalled more negative words while those who learned in a happy state recalled more positive words.[15] Similar effects have also been shown using mood states altered by exposure to different types of music and inducing mood changes via self-reference statements aimed at raising or lowering mood.[16]

Once again, however, we must be cautious in attributing a large role to emotional factors in everyday remembering. The experiments have gone to extreme lengths to induce polarised mood changes in people and, generally speaking, these variations in mood are not characteristic of the population. Thus they show the potential of mood to affect memory rather than demonstrate a pervasive effect central to everyday remembering. Also some have made use of hypnosis—a technique we will criticise in Chapter 7. A different picture emerges if we consider clinical depression in which the patient has an abnormal level of sadness. A feature of depression is that it varies in its intensity and this fact was exploited in a study which examined the recall of depressed people at different points in their mood swings. At points where the patients were relatively happy their recollections were also positive but, as their depression worsened, the frequency of negative memories increased. Here, then, emotional state is a critical factor in determining memory.[17]

REMEMBERING WITHOUT AWARENESS

So far we have been dealing with what one could term conscious remembering in that all the forms of memory we have considered involve people being consciously aware that they are remembering something. Intuitively you might think that all memory involves this kind of remembering but you would be wrong—there is now good evidence that people may often remember things without realising.

Consider the following demonstration experiment. First you view a series of target words such as ANEMONE, CATERPILLAR, DUNGEON, and I ask you to remember them. A day later I give you two tests. The first is a straightforward recognition test in which you have to identify the words I showed you the day before. The other test makes no reference to the previous day but just asks you to do a word puzzle in which you must fill in blanks to make a word, e.g. _NE_O_E, _ER_U_E, _UN_E_N, _SS_SS_N. You will notice that the answer to the first and third fragments are words that you were asked to remember whereas the other two solutions are not. The outcome of this type of study is that fragments corresponding to targets are completed more successfully. You may not find this surprising because, after all, subjects must be able to remember the list and it is this that helps them do the fragment completion test. Unfortunately the explanation of this finding is not so simple for two reasons. First, if subjects are using their recollection of the word list to help them then it follows that they should be more successful at solving fragments corresponding to words they remember. This is not the case, thus suggesting that conscious recollection is not involved.[18]

Psychologists use the term **priming** to describe the type of memory underlying better completion of fragments corresponding to target words. Priming represents one instance of a more general class of memory phenomena known as **implicit memory**. Sometimes called **indirect memory**, implicit memory refers to any test of memory in which aspects of the individual's past influence his or her performance even though the person is not necessarily aware of this. Thus in fragment completion subjects are not always aware that a successful solution relates to a word they were asked to remember the day before. Implicit memory is contrasted with **explicit memory**—which relates to what we typically associate the word "remembering" with, i.e. the conscious recall or recognition of information from memory.[19]

The findings of implicit memory research are very clear; in many instances we are being influenced by our past experiences without being aware of it. The implications of this important discovery are far reaching, particularly in relation to advertising. A typical assumption about the effectiveness of adverts is that they exert their effect by evoking some form of conscious recollection on the part of the individual. Thus millions are spent on trying to make adverts as amusing and the distinctive as possible in the hope that they will be remembered and thus consciously influence the purchaser. However, is it true that adverts actually work in this way? A number of studies have explored the memorability of adverts and the results are not particularly encouraging for the conscious memorability theory. In one study subjects were exposed to an advert for 13 weeks but six weeks later only 20% were able to recall it. Studies like this allow two possible conclusions: either adverts are simply unmemorable or they exert their effects in ways other than via conscious remembering.[20]

There is now good evidence that adverts may exert their effects implicitly. In one experiment subjects were shown adverts in colour magazines. One group were asked to look at them directly and rate how attractive they were. The other group encountered the same adverts incidentally in that they were directed to read parts of the article to which the advert was adjacent. About five minutes later subjects were tested on how well they remembered the pictures using a recognition test and all subjects were also asked to rate the attractiveness of the adverts. The group who had deliberately studied the adverts recognised more of them correctly but of more interest was the finding that there was no difference in the extent to which both groups rated the previously exposed adverts as more attractive. This study thus suggests that our implicit memory for adverts may have motivating effects that we are not consciously aware of. Given the highly specific nature of these effects much more subtle and targeted manipulations may be possible. The power of advertising should not be underestimated.[21]

IMPLICIT LEARNING

Implicit learning refers to situations in which people know they have been through a learning experience but cannot articulate what they have learned. An example of this is the so-called sugar production task in which subjects are presented with a computer simulation of a sugar production factory. Their task is to maximise output by balancing the amount of raw materials used against the number of workers. The program operates according to a particular rule. Most subjects are able to optimise output of the simulated factory but few are able to say what the rule is. Similar effects have been observed in many other similar situations and show that quite complex learning can be achieved without conscious involvement.[22]

UNCONSCIOUS LEARNING

The experiments we considered in the pervious section showed that people show evidence of remembering when they are not aware of it. This should not be construed as evidence that learning can occur without consciousness. In all the studies we considered subjects were fully alert during the learning phase—the crucial finding was that aspects of the learning influenced subjects subsequently without them realising or without them being able to recollect what they had learned.

It is a very different matter to suggest that people can learn when they are not conscious, but many claims of this type have been made. At the top of the list is **sleep learning**, in which it is claimed that people can study information while asleep and successfully recall it when awake. During the 1980s the US Army invested a large amount of money into researching various "New Age" abilities such as remote viewing and tele-kinesis. Inevitably they examined sleep learning and their conclusions were simple: There was no evidence for sleep learning and, in those instances where claims for sleep learning had been made, the subjects were most likely awake.[23]

A more important issue is whether people can learn information while they are under the influence of an anaesthetic. There are, of course, many people who claim this occurs and quite a few have successfully sued for damages due to the stress caused. So what is the truth about memory in anaesthesia? In a study of dubious ethical quality a dental surgeon staged a mock crisis during an operation which, among other things, referred to the patient going blue due to lack of oxygen. On awakening no subject recalled the incident but, when hypnotised, several subjects recalled the event.[24] We have already raised concerns about the use of hypnosis so better evidence is needed if we are to believe that anaesthesia allows learning to occur. A number of these studies have involved implicit memory by showing, for example, that given a category label after the operation (e.g. fruits) previously anaesthetised patients were more likely to give examples which were played to them during the operation than examples which were not.[25] There are, however, additional claims that subjects can have explicit memory for information presented during an operation although this appears less reliable. On the surface it seems that memories can be formed during anaesthesia but we must be cautious. Anaesthesia is a difficult procedure and it is inevitable that some people may briefly go in and out of consciousness during an operation. Events like this may be sufficient to account for much apparent learning during anaesthesia.[26]

FORGETTING

The systematic study of forgetting was initiated by the German psychologist Hermann Ebbinghaus, who published his work in 1885. Ebbinghaus believed that memory could only be studied accurately by requiring subjects to learn information they were unfamiliar with. If familiar material was used then the results would be contaminated by individuals using their own knowledge in differing degrees as a means of helping them remember.[7] Ebbinghaus devised the nonsense syllable (e.g. TOK) as his basis for exploring memory. He worked mainly on himself by reading out lists of these nonsense syllables and then measuring how well he remembered them. Because the lists were usually quite long he would require several recitations before perfect recall. To examine forgetting he attempted to learn the same lists again at different points in time.

The first important finding was that relearning lists was usually quicker than the previous learning. This is known as **savings** and indicates that, even though we may not be able to recall something consciously, we have some information about it stored away which can help us relearn more quickly. The second point was that the amount of savings observed declined as the time interval increased. Figure 2.1 shows the nature of this forgetting—it shows that forgetting is initially very rapid with half the information forgotten within 20 minutes. Forgetting then becomes a very gradual process, with two-thirds lost after two days and 80% within a month.

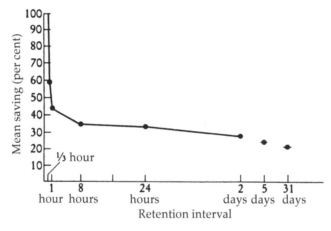

Figure 2.1: Forgetting rate, as measured by Ebbinghaus. Note how most forgetting occurs very soon after learning.

Why Does Forgetting Occur?

Forgetting can occur for a number of reasons. In this chapter we have already seen many examples of forgetting arising from **retrieval failure** in that the information required is in memory but unavailable because, for example, there has been a change of context or mood. This chapter has also illustrated the central role of encoding in memory—if information is not meaningfully encoded it will not be well remembered (**encoding failure**). However, the third and perhaps most pervasive form of forgetting is **storage failure**. We can think of storage failure occurring in two ways: *either* there is **consolidation failure**, as might occur in someone who was suddenly shocked or highly intoxicated, *or* there is some disruption to the memory once it has been transferred to LTS.

The influence of shock on memory is nicely demonstrated in a study which examined how well two groups of students remembered a set of nonsense words. After the learning phase one group were allowed to rest and given a joke book to read. The other group suffered a series of unexpected mishaps which involved chairs collapsing, metal falling from the ceiling, a gun going off, electric shocks, and a power failure. When recall was tested the group who suffered the disruptions were somewhat shattered and remembered far less than those who read the joke book. In this study, which one would not dare to repeat, one can presume that the unexpected events distracted and stressed the students thus interfering with the biological mechanisms of consolidation.

Studies of this kind show, *in extremis*, how external factors might disrupt the consolidation process. However, it is likely that the consolidation process frequently fails without any drastic interventions of this type. Look again at Figure 2.1 which shows the extremely rapid forgetting observed by Ebbinghaus in the period immediately after learning. There is good reason to suppose that this rapid decline in memory represents a failure to consolidate information in LTS. It is known that the formation of permanent memory depends crucially on the process of protein synthesis. Various drugs are known to inhibit protein synthesis and studies of animals show that when these drugs are injected within half an hour of learning there is severe disruption to memory. However, when given an hour later, memory is unaffected. It seems, therefore, that the process of consolidation is occurring during the same period that Ebbinghaus observed rapid forgetting.

Forgetting in LTS

How might memories in LTS become disrupted? One popular idea is the so-called "Law of Disuse" which states that memories decay with time unless they are used. The problem with this theory is that time itself cannot be an explanation of anything. Something is happening to a memory during the time it is not being used and it this we must explain. One theory is that there is simply a biological "wearing out" process in that failure to use the memory leads to a deterioration in the synaptic connections responsible for the memory. While we cannot completely rule this out it seems unlikely. In his influential book *Awakenings*, Oliver Sachs describes people who awoke after being in a sleep-like state for many years due to the illness encephalitis lethargica. A fascinating feature of these people was their extremely good recall of events in their lives prior to their illness—something we would not expect if continued use of memories was necessary to prevent forgetting.

The above point is emphasised in a more controlled way in a classic experiment conducted in the 1920s. People learned a list of nonsense words either late at night or early in the morning and were then tested after intervals ranging from one to eight hours later. The results were clear cut: those subjects who slept during the period between learning and test forgot far less than those who were awake. If memories were lost simply by a time-based decay process we would not expect to see more forgetting in the group that stayed awake. The fact that being awake disrupted memory more suggested that the intervening activities carried out while awake somehow **interfered** with what the people had learned.

The idea that memory can be disrupted by interference is now widely accepted and two forms can be identified. When the learning of new information is prevented by information you have learned previously it is called **proactive interference**. Conversely, when new information prevents the recall of previously learned information it is called **retroactive interference**. These terms are best remembered using practical examples. Calling your second wife by the name of your first wife is a particularly embarrassing form of proactive interference, and failing to remember what you had for your 20th birthday present might be attributed to retroactive interference from presents given on subsequent birthdays.

It is important to note that information apparently lost by interference can resurface at a later point—a process known as **spontaneous recovery**. Early in my career I was once the not-so-proud owner of a Hillman Hunter which was unusual for a British car in that the hand brake was on the right. My subsequent cars have all had the hand brake on the left and you would think that by now all that competing information would have completely obliterated any memory of the hand brake being on the right. However, on occasion, particularly when I am in a tight situation, I have mistakenly used my right hand to reach for the hand brake. This example shows that when memories are interfered with they are not so much lost as suppressed and, as such, may reappear at a subsequent point in time.

SUMMARY

- The idea of total recall is a myth: memory is a selective process.
- Remembering involves a process of reconstruction.
- Reconstruction is thought to make use of schemata: general frameworks about the world in which we operate.
- Recognition can be based on either familiarity or recollection.
- Context refers to the information associated with what we are trying to remember: if it is intimately related to the target information it is known as intrinsic context; if it is incidental it is known as extrinsic context.
- The influence of psychoactive state on memory is known as state-dependent learning.
- Emotion influences memory: memories consistent with our mood are easier to remember than those which are not.
- Implicit memory refers to memory processes which influence us without our realising it. Explicit memory, in contrast, is deliberate recollection of the past.

- It is not possible to learn while asleep.
- Forgetting can arise through encoding failure, storage failure, or retrieval failure.
- Forgetting does not occur simply because we do not use a given memory. Forgetting seems to be due to some form of interference.
- Apparently forgotten memories can return due to spontaneous recovery.

NOTES AND REFERENCES

1. Penfield, W. (1958) Some mechanisms of consciousness discovered during electrical stimulation of the brain. *Proceedings of the National Academy of Sciences*, **44**, 51–66.
2. Loftus, E.F. & Loftus, G.R. (1980) On the permanence of stored information in the brain. *American Psychologist*, **35**, 409–420.
3. Experiments like this were the basis of the "levels of processing" approach to memory which was seen as an alternative to thinking about memory as STS and LTS. For an account see Parkin, A.J. (1993) *Memory: Phenomena, Experiment and Theory*, chap. 2. Oxford: Basil Blackwell.
4. De Groot, A.D. (1966) Perception and memory vs thought. In B. Kleimuntz (ed.), *Problem Solving*. New York: Wiley.
5. James, W. (1889) *Talks to Teachers on Psychology*. New York: Holt.
6. Schank, R.C. & Abelson, R.P. (1977) *Scripts, Plans, Goals, and Understanding*. Hillsdale, NJ: Lawrence Erlbaum. See also: Baddeley, A.D. (1997) *Human Memory: Theory and Practice*, pp. 244–250. Hove: Psychology Press. Eysenck, M.W. & Keane M.T. (1995) *Cognitive Psychology: A Student's Handbook*, pp. 261–270. Hove: Psychology Press.
7. Bartlett, F.C. (1932) *Remembering: A Study in Experimental and Social Psychology*. Cambridge: Cambridge University Press.

8. Neisser, U. (1982) John Dean's Memory. In U. Neisser (ed.) *Memory Observed*, pp. 139–159. San Francisco: Freeman.
9. This idea originates with Mandler, G. (1980) Recognising: the judgement of a previous occurrence. *Psychological Review*, **27**, 252–271.
10. Godden, D. & Baddeley, A.D. (1975) Context-dependent memory in two natural environments: on land and under water. *British Journal of Psychology*, **66**, 325–331.
11. Smith, S.M. (1979) Remembering in and out of context. *Journal of Experimental Psychology: Human Learning and Memory*, **5**, 460–471.
12. Eich, J.E. (1980) The cue-dependent nature of state-dependent retrieval. *Memory & Cognition*, **8**, 157–173. While most studies of state-dependent learning have used psychoactive substances, the phenomenon may be more widespread. Recently it has been shown that information learned during aerobic exercise is recalled better during subsequent similar exercise than when at rest. See Miles, C. & Daylen, J. (1998) State dependent memory produced by aerobic exercise. *Ergonomics*, **41**, 20–28.
13. Block, R.I. & Wittenborn, J.R. (1985) Marijuana effects on associative processes. *Psychopharmacology*, **85**, 426–430.
14. Bower, G. et al. (1981) Selectivity of learning caused by affective state. *Journal of Experimental Psychology*, **110**, 451–473.
15. Rinck, M. et al. (1992) Mood-congruent and mood-incongruent learning. *Memory and Cognition*, **20**, 29–39.
16. Kenealy, P.M. (1997) Mood-state-dependent retrieval: The effects of induced mood on memory reconsidered. *Quarterly Journal of Experimental Psychology*, **50A**, 290–317.
17. Williams, J.M.G. et al. (1995) *Cognitive Psychology and Emotional Disorders*. Chichester: Wiley. See also Mineka, S. & Nugent, K. (1995) Mood-congruent memory biases in anxiety and depression. In D.L. Schacter et al. (eds) *Memory Distortions: How Minds, Brains, and Societies Reconstruct the Past*, pp. 173–193. Cambridge, MA: Harvard University Press.
18. Tulving, E., Schacter, D.L. & Stark, H.A. (1982) Priming effects in word fragment completion are independent of

recognition memory. *Journal of Experimental Psychology: Learning, Memory & Cognition*, **8**, 336–342.

19. Graf, P. & Schacter, D.L. (1985) Implicit and explicit memory for new associations in normal and amnesic subjects. *Journal of Experimental Psychology: Learning, Memory & Cognition*, **13**, 45–53.

20. Zielske, H.A. (1959) The remembering and forgetting of advertising. *Journal of Marketing*, **23**, 239–243.

21. Perfect, T. & Askew, C. (1994) Print adverts: Not remembered but memorable. *Applied Cognitive Psychology*, **8**, 693–703.

22. There has been a lot of recent work in this area. A good overview is provided by Berry, D.C. & Dienes, Z. (1996) *Implicit and Explicit Learning in Human Performance*. Hove: Psychology Press.

23. Bjork, R.A. et al. (eds) (1994) *Learning, Remembering, Believing: Enhancing Human Performance*. Report of the National Research Council. Committee on Techniques for the Enhancement of Human Performance. Washington: National Academy.

24. Levinson, B.W. (1965) States of awareness during general anaesthesia. *British Journal of Psychology*, **37**, 544–546.

25. Jelcic, M. et al. (1992) Implicit memory for words presented during anaesthesia. *European Journal of Cognitive Psychology*, **4**, 71–80.

26. A good recent review of anaesthetic effects and memory is provided by Andrade, J. (1995) Learning during anaesthesia: A review. *British Journal of Psychology*, **86**, 479–506. See also Bonebakker, A.E. et al. (1996) Memory during general anesthesia: Practical and methodological aspects. *Consciousness and Cognition*, **5** 542–561. Bonke, B. et al. (eds) (1990) *Memory and Awareness in Anaesthesia 3*. Assen, Netherlands: Van Gorcum & Co B.V.

3

MEMORY ACROSS THE LIFESPAN

How far back can you remember? Some people claim to re-member events from very early childhood and some even re-member being born. In this chapter we will track the development of memory from the moment of birth (or even before) through to old age. You will find that memory develops very early but that recollection of those early memories is not possible in later life.

EARLY LEARNING

According to some studies learning actually begins before babies are born. Thus, in one study it was shown that new-born infants respond more readily to their mother's voice.[1] From birth onwards there is plenty of evidence that even very young infants can learn and remember although you may be wondering how to establish that a child of less than a year old remembers anything because it cannot, of course, speak. Various ingenious ways have nonetheless been devised to show that young infants do remember at an early age. One technique is known as **novelty preference** and exploits the fact that infants older than 10 weeks will tend to look longer at something that is novel than something that has been seen before. So, if shown two things, one novel and one pre-exposed, an infant that looks longer at the novel item can be assumed to remember the pre-exposed item. An experiment using 1-day-old children repeatedly presented a checkerboard pattern which gradually the infants looked at less and less. At this point a novel checkerboard was introduced and gaze times increased—thus indicating some form of memory for the original checkerboard.[2] Generally experiments with the novelty preference technique have shown that memories formed in the early stages of life are short-lived. However, one study involving infants between 2 and 5 months showed that these preferences can last over a day, with the effects being stronger in older infants.[3]

Intuitively one might expect learning processes already present in an infant to be relatively primitive and reflect those learning mechanisms shared with lower animals. **Classical conditioning** was discovered by Pavlov and refers to a process in which a previously neutral stimulus—the **conditioned stimulus (CS)**—can become associated with a response that can already be elicited by another stimulus known as the **unconditioned stimulus (US)**. Pavlov demonstrated this by showing that the natural salivation reflex associated with food—**unconditioned response (UR)**—could become associated with the ringing of a bell, providing the bell and food were paired. A **conditioned response (CR)** was said to have occurred when the bell caused salivation without the food being present.[4]

In infants psychologists have examined conditioning of the **eyeblink reflex** in which initially a CS (tone) was paired with an air puff to the eye (US) which elicited an eyeblink response (UR). Across time a CR is developed in which the tone leads to an eyeblink without the US being present. Using this technique it was found that infants as young as 20 days could retain the conditioned response.[5]

The other form of conditioning is **operant conditioning**. In operant conditioning a voluntary response meets with some pleasant occurrence and is therefore **reinforced** to occur again in the same situation. Thus if a rat presses a bar and receives food this response will recur.[4] Operant conditioning has been used in an ingenious way to investigate learning in infants. Essentially a mobile is placed above the infant with a tape attaching it to the infant's ankle (see Figure 3.1). The infant soon learns that kicking causes the mobile to move and this movement serves to reinforce the kicking response. The mobiles comprised distinctive visual information and it was assumed that the infants would learn something about this information. To test this out they were, after a delay, presented with either the same mobile or a different one. Experiments have repeatedly shown that infants more readily kick when the mobile is the same than when it is changed. The length of time for which this can be remembered increases significantly during infanthood.[6]

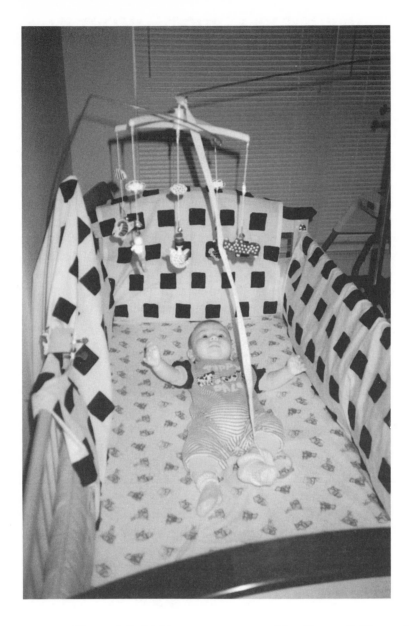

Figure 3.1: The mobile kicking apparatus used by Rovee-Collier and her colleagues. (Photograph courtesy of C. Rovee-Collier.)

IMPLICIT VS EXPLICIT MEMORY IN CHILDREN

In Chapter 2 we saw that there are important differences between memory tasks that make implicit or explicit demands on
adults. The same applies with children. In an experiment I carried out with Sarah Streete[7] we showed 3-, 5-, 7-year-olds and
adults sequences of degraded pictures (see Figure 3.2). The most
degraded version was shown first followed by more informative
versions of the pictures until identification was established.
After a delay the picture sequences were repeated to establish
whether the subjects now needed less information to identify the
pictures, i.e. achieved correct identification with a less informative picture than before. Children as young as 3 years old
showed learning in these circumstances even though, in the case
of the 3-year-olds, their ability to remember having seen the
pictures before (explicit memory) was very poor.

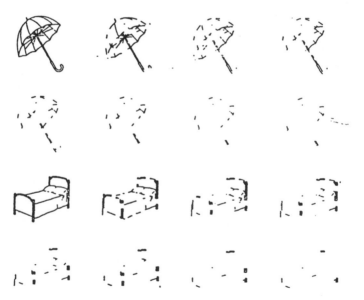

Figure 3.2: Examples of pictures used by Parkin and Streete.

Minimally our experiment showed that implicit memory can occur in children as young as 3. A more problematic issue is whether implicit memory develops further from that point. Some studies have argued that implicit memory does not change with age whereas others argue that there is a strong developmental trend. One problem is that the implicit task, picture naming, can be "contaminated" by the individual's ability to remember seeing certain objects during the learning phase (e.g. "I remember there was an umbrella"). It is therefore possible that apparent age effects in implicit memory reflect older children's greater ability to remember the presentation episode. A recent study similar to the one I carried out with Streete takes account of this and finds no evidence of developmental trend.[8]

MEMORY UP TO THE AGE OF 4

Why should there be something special about the age of 4? The answer lies in the phenomenon of **infantile amnesia**. This refers to the fact that we can remember little if anything of events occurring before this time.[9] Because of this it was, until recently, widely believed that the ability to recall specific events (explicit memory) below the age of 4 was either very poor or non-existent. However, more recent evidence has suggested that younger children can remember quite a lot. Consider this conversation with a child who is not quite 3 years of age:

CHILD: *Once on Halloween the kids was over and I had a princess dress on me.*
ADULT: *You had a princess dress on? Did you get any candy? Did you go door to door? What happened?*
CHILD: *We went treating.*
ADULT: *You went treating! and who took you?*
CHILD: *Andrea's mother took us. And my mom . . . and we brought a pumpkin too.*

ADULT: *What did you do with the pumpkin?*
CHILD: *We lighted it.*
ADULT: *What did it look like? Was it scary?*
CHILD: *Uh-huh. Dad made cuts in it with a razor. He made a*
         face too. That was funny.[10]

Other studies have shown, for example, that very young children can give detailed accounts of events like going to McDonald's or visiting Disneyworld and that they differ from older children simply in the amount of detail they remember.[11] However, other researchers have been less impressed with these findings and have queried the fact that a great deal of the information recalled by these young children is in response to prompts and directed questioning—as shown in the above quote.

Doubts over the use of verbal measures have led to the use of non-verbal tasks as a way of showing that children under 4 can remember specific events. Two tasks in particular have been used: **object hiding** and **elicited imitation**. In object hiding the child watches an adult hide an object and then, after a delay, the child is allowed to look for it. If the child remembers the location of the object then some memory for the hiding event must be present. Diamond[12] made use of this ability using a task known as **delayed non-matching to sample.** This sounds complicated but is actually very easy. At the start of a trial the child is shown an object and learns that by picking it up it can earn a reward (e.g. a sweet). The object is then obscured and, after a delay, two objects are revealed. In order to achieve a reward this time the child must lift up the object they did not see previously for a reward—thus requiring that they remember the original object. Children of 21 months can manage this task well and retain the information for about 30 seconds.

Elicited imitation involves the use of props to model an action which the child is then asked to imitate at a later point. Depending on the age of the child the event may involve a single action or multiple actions. Using this technique it has been shown that infants as young as 11 months can accurately imitate familiar events (e.g. putting a teddy bear to bed) and novel events (e.g.

using a button and a box to produce a rattle). Across the first two and half years of life children show a steady increase in the sequences of events that they can remember, with the oldest group being able to remember eight step sequences. There are also age effects in the length of time that children can remember information about these imitated events: 9-month-olds retain information for 24 hours, 14-month-olds still remember the sequences after a week and by 20 months recall is still evident for intervals up to six weeks.[13]

Infantile Amnesia

Before leaving this section we must briefly reconsider infantile amnesia. There have been many attempts to explain why this phenomenon occurs. Freud considered it as evidence of repression because, according to his psycho-sexual theory of development (see Chapter 7, pp. 143–144) it was during the early years of life that the conflicts involved in his theory took place. However, virtually nobody takes this account seriously and the infantile amnesia period is now thought to reflect the way memories are represented. Having said that, there is little agreement beyond this point. One idea, however, relates to the idea of **autobiographical memory**[14]—this is a proposed subsystem of declarative memory which deals specifically with personal experiences and in some way gives memories the property of having personally involved us. This property is essential for recollection to occur and it has been argued that memories formed before the age of 4 lack this quality and this is why, if recalled at all, they require a great deal of prompting.[15] An alternative idea is that, as memory develops, it acquires more of a narrative quality and that memories formed with little or no narrative structure are difficult to recall because the later memory system looks for narrative structure as the basis for autobiographical recall.[16]

MEMORY BEYOND THE AGE OF 4

After the age of 4 memory shows a steady increase in efficiency with older children showing better performance on tests of recall and recognition memory. There are a number of reasons why this increase takes place. A very influential factor is the development of **memory strategies**—which can be defined as any effortful mental operation that serves to enhance memory. One of the most fundamental memory strategies is **rehearsal**, which involves the repetition of information you are trying to remember. An early American study showed that 85% of children in the 5th grade used rehearsal as a strategy when trying to remember compared with only 10% in kindergarten. Other studies have not found differences in the proportion of children of different ages who use rehearsal, but older children rehearse more information at a time.[17]

Organisation is another factor that underlies developmental increases in memory. This refers to the fact that material can be made easier to remember by imposing some form of meaningful organisation on it. There are many demonstrations that younger children make less use of organisational strategies when remembering. If children are given a list of words which, although randomly arranged, contains words from specific categories (e.g. fruits, animals) then older children will make more use of the organisational potential by recalling the words category by category. Organisational strategies based on meaning are not used spontaneously until children are around 9–10 years of age.[18]

Retrieval strategies also vary with age. In one study 1st-, 3rd-, and 6th-grade children were asked to learn three small pictures from each of eight categories and it was ensured that the children knew that the items came from the various categories. This was done by linking the small pictures with a large "linking" picture (e.g. three animal pictures might be linked to the "zoo" concept represented by three empty cages). At test the large pictures were presented as cues. With no cues there was a standard increase in recall with age. When the large pictures were presented as cues only the sixth-grade children showed enhanced memory. However, when a "directive cue" was used, in which the children were told how many small pictures went with each large picture, recall improved in all groups and there was no age difference.[19] This latter finding, confirmed in other studies, indicates that differences in retrieval are not due to differential learning of the material but due to differences in implementing effective retrieval strategies.

WHAT IS DEVELOPING?

There are many factors that may contribute to the development of a child's memory. One factor relates to the idea of **processing resources**. The basis of this idea is there is only a certain amount of neural capacity available for memory and that this grows as the brain matures. One way to think of capacity is in terms of the development of STS—the idea being that the capacity of STS directly determines the extent to which we can deal with information and, for example, allocate particular processing strategies. There are many studies showing that the capacity of STS, as measured by digit span or related tasks, increases with age and this serves as a fruitful basis for thinking about memory development in terms of the quantity of memory capacity available.[20]

An alternative, and more qualitative, view about memory development involves schemata which we encountered in Chapter 2. Briefly schemata, or **scripts** as they are sometimes called, are generalised descriptions we build up of events. Studies have shown that younger children have less specific schemata which, in turn, means that they are less likely to remember any deviation from the norm in a particular sequence of events.[21] This was illustrated in an experiment where children of different ages went to an activity room and were invited to play a standard set of games by an adult dressed as a particular animal. Three such visits were made followed by a deviation visit in which the adult was dressed as a different animal. Later questioning showed that younger children were less able to distinguish the standard from the deviation visit. The explanation was that young children's schemata only specified that "there was an adult dressed as an animal" without any additional information that the animal could vary.[22]

The concept of schemata is inextricably linked to the idea that knowledge *per se* plays a crucial role in memory development. One nice demonstration of this was a study which compared children of 7, 9, and 11 on a recall task for categorically organised items or their classmates. As expected, recall of the categorised list increased with age—something we can attribute to increased knowledge allowing the easier application of an organisational strategy. However, there was no difference in the recall of classmates where, presumably, the degree of knowledge was similar.[23]

Metamemory is a term which reflects our knowledge about how memory works. Metamemory has been assessed using questionnaires which ask children various questions about how memory works.[24] One question, for example, examines whether children appreciate that some people have better or worse memories than they have. Nine- and 11-year-olds understood this, but kindergarten subjects tended to think they had better memories than their friends and 30% thought they never forgot anything. The questionnaire also confirmed younger children's lesser ability to appreciate the value of categorical knowledge in remembering and that younger children were poorer at devising strategies for remembering to do something. The poorer memory of younger children is, at least in part, explicable in terms of their poor ideas about how memory works.

MEMORY LATER IN LIFE

Most studies of adult memory involve the use of college students, so the results and theories derived from this research really relate to young adults. Interestingly there is very little research on memory during later working life although evidence exists that significant declines in memory are apparent in 40- and 50-year-olds. In some ways this is unfortunate because it is around this time that many people's careers take on a big memory load. Bill Clinton, for example, in his defence over his affair with Monica Lewinski, claimed that he forgot details of his various encounters with her because his memory was overloaded!

Research into memory in later life have thus concentrated on retired people—the post-65 age bracket. A number of robust findings have emerged from this literature. The first concerns the nature of STS function which remains largely unaffected by advancing age. Digit span, for example, changes little if at all as we get older. Generally knowledge about the world and vocabulary remains intact although there is evidence that older people access their memories more slowly.[25]

The major change in memory with age is a decline in the ability to recall things explicitly. Thus memory for day-to-day events decreases markedly and, in the laboratory, we find older people performing much more poorly when asked to recall lists of words or pictures.[26] An interesting feature of ageing is that recognition memory does not decline so drastically and there have been claims that recognition memory does not deteriorate with age. This latter conclusion is not true on two counts. First, as people get older their ability to know that they have seen something, e.g. a face, does not decline but there is an increase in the tendency to think they have seen somebody when they have not. One study for example showed that young and old subjects did not differ on detecting faces they had seen but older subjects were much more likely to falsely identify lookalikes as well.[27]

The second age-linked feature of recognition memory is that it changes subjectively with age. You will have had the experience of encountering people in the street and finding their faces familiar yet be unable to recall their names or anything about them. Within the jargon of psychology this would described as finding someone **familiar** but failing to place that person in any **context**. There is good evidence that as we grow older our recognition memory becomes more "familiarity-based". In an experiment I conducted with Brenda Walter[28] we showed young and old people lists of words. A recognition test then followed in which they had to identify which words on a bigger list were ones that had just been presented. In addition we also sought information about how they were identifying the words. After each identification we asked them to indicate whether they "remembered" the word or merely found it "familiar". A remember response was one in which the person remembered some specific context about the word when it was originally presented, e.g. that it followed another word, or reminded them of something. Alternatively, they could just indicate that the word was familiar, i.e. that they think it was presented but have no context to base this decision on (this was termed a "know" response). The results showed that, as age increased, familiarity-based responding went up and remember-based responding went down.

IMPLICIT MEMORY AND AGEING

In our discussion of children's memory we saw that there was evidence that implicit memory was in place before explicit memory developed and, furthermore, that implicit memory ability may remain unchanged during development. It is therefore of interest that implicit memory appears intact in older people in contrast to explicit memory which, as we saw, declines markedly with age—it is as if memory development operates on a "first in–last out" principle. This contrast is neatly illustrated in an experiment that compared cued recall, a test of explicit memory, with **stem completion**, a test of implicit memory.[29] Stem completion is a task similar to fragment completion (see Chapter 2) in which words are initially exposed followed by a test in which subjects are shown the first few letters of a word and asked to complete the stem with the first word that comes to mind. Typical subjects are much more likely to complete the stems with previously exposed words (e.g. shown REASON they are much more likely to complete REA_? as REASON). The neat aspect of stem completion is that the stems can also be used as cues for explicit memory, e.g. which word in the list you saw began with REA? When old and young subjects are compared on the implicit version of the task there is no difference in performance but, when exactly the same cues are used for explicit recall there is a big age difference.

Other studies have, however, suggested that implicit memory deteriorates with age. However, a study I carried out with Riccardo Russo[30] indicates that apparent age effects in implicit memory may occur because older subjects make less use of their explicit memory at test. We used the same incomplete picture series that we had used with the children (see Figure 3.2). Initial analysis indicated a big age effect with younger subjects showing more evidence of implicit memory. However, when we took into account how much subjects remembered the pictures and based our analysis only on non-remembered pictures there was no age effect. This indicates that it is the younger subjects' superior explicit memory that accounts for the apparent age difference in implicit memory.

A question I am often asked is "Can I do anything to stop my memory getting poorer as I get older?" Studies of animals do suggest that an enriched environment results in the loss of fewer neurones as age progresses, so it is reasonable to assume the same in humans. However, there is not a great deal of evidence on this. Nonetheless, a few studies have compared elderly individuals living in institutionalised settings with those living more active lives in the community. On various tests of memory the active community-dwelling elderly have better memories.[31] The message, therefore, seems to be: keep mentally active.

WHAT DECLINES WITH AGE?

At the simplest level our memories fail increasingly with age because we lose neurones. In particular we lose them from the

frontal lobes and the hippocampal region—both areas intimately related to memory.[32] However, psychologists go one
step further and attempt to explain what neuronal loss means in
psychological terms. As with memory development, processing
capacity has been put forward as an explanation with increased
age resulting in a reduction of processing resources. However,
unlike with children, it has been harder to find an easy measure
of processing resources because STS function does not decline
with age. An alternative idea relates to the concept of **inhibition**.[33] In order to function effectively it is assumed that our
mental processes must attend to what we are doing and actively
ignore irrelevant information. In relation to memory a deficit in
inhibition could impair memory, leading people to concentrate
less effectively on what they are trying to learn or remember.
Furthermore, the inhibition idea gets further support from the
fact that ageing selectively causes cell neurone depletion in the
frontal lobes: we know from studies of brain-damaged people
that the frontal lobes contain the mental mechanisms responsible for inhibition.

Perhaps the most popular theory of ageing and memory is
that our memories get poorer because our brains just get
slower at operating. This **processing speed** hypothesis[34] gains
support from studies in which age effects in memory are obtained and then related to non-memory-based measures of processing speed such as deciding whether two designs are similar
or not. Statistics are then used to see if the age differences in
memory can be explained by age differences in the processing
speed task. This approach has yielded a large amount of evidence that age-related changes in memory, as well as some
other declines in mental capacity, seem to be accounted for by
simple slowing down of the brain. There is, however, a problem with this explanation. It assumes that the processing speed
tasks used are so simple that they are effectively measuring the
velocity of basic neural activity. Unfortunately, recent work
has shown that these tasks, although apparently simple, may
be measuring higher level function, particularly **fluid
intelligence**—a form of intelligence that represents our ability
to think flexibly, solve problems, etc., and is contrasted with

crystallised intelligence, which is our knowledge of language and basic concepts. Fluid intelligence is known to decline markedly with age and it may be this that underlies age-related memory loss.[35]

SUMMARY

- There is some indication that children can learn in the womb.
- From a very early age children can learn through the process of conditioning.
- Implicit memory develops before explicit memory. There is some suggestion that implicit memory does not vary with age.
- Infantile amnesia refers to our inability to recollect events before the age of about 4.
- Children can recall events before age 4, but their memory is more reliably demonstrated using non-verbal measures.
- A key feature of memory development is that older children become more efficient at using memory strategies.
- Various factors contribute to memory development, including: greater processing resources, better knowledge as reflected in more complex schemata, and better metamemory.
- When we get older it is principally our ability to remember events that declines. STS and implicit memory are largely unaffected.
- The age-related decline in recollection is linked to a failure to remember context.
- The two most common explanations of ageing are that it arises through a decline in inhibitory mechanisms or from a decline in processing speed.

NOTES AND REFERENCES

1. There are two studies relevant here: De Casper and Spence
    showed that young infants preferred to attend to stories
    their mother's had read to them while they were in the
    room as opposed to other stories read to them by their
    mother (De Casper, A.J. & Fifer, W.P. (1980) Of human
    bonding: Newborns prefer their mothers' voices. *Science*,
    208, 1174–1176.) Obviously the infants could not under-
    stand the stories; it was the sound patterns they recognised.
    The second study showed that infants sucked harder on an
    artificial nipple when reinforced with the sound of their
    mother's voice (De Casper, A.J. & Spence, M.J. (1986) Pre-
    natal maternal speech influences newborns' perception of
    speech sounds. *Infant Behaviour and Development*, **9**, 133–
    150.) There are also apparent accounts that babies whose
    mothers listened to "Neighbours" during pregnancy
    showed less interest in the theme tune than babies whose
    mothers were not "Neighbours" fans.
2. Friedman, S. (1972) Newborn visual attention to repeated
    exposure of redundant vs "novel" targets. *Perception and
    Psychophysics*, **12**, 291–294.
3. Martin, R.M. (1975) Effects of familiar and complex stimuli
    on infant attention. *Developmental Psychology*, **11**, 178–185.
4. Although published some time ago, a good introduction to
    conditioning is Rachlin, H. (1976) *A Guide to Modern Be-
    haviourism*. San Francisco: Freeman.
5. Little, A.H. et al. (1984) Classical conditioning and reten-
    tion of the infant's eyelid response. Effects of age and inter-
    stimulus interval. *Journal of Experimental Child Psychology*,
    37, 512–524.
6. Rovee-Collier, C. & Gerhardstein, P. (1997) The develop-
    ment of infant memory. In N. Cowan (ed.) *The Development
    of Memory in Childhood*. Hove: Psychology Press.
7. Parkin, A.J. & Streete, S. (1988) Implicit and explicit mem-
    ory in young children and adults. *British Journal of Psychol-
    ogy*, **79**, 361–369.

8. Russo, R. et al. (1995) Developmental trends in implicit and explicit memory: A picture completion study. *Journal of Experimental Child Psychology*, **59**, 566–578. But see Rovee-Collier, C. (1997) Dissociations in infant memory: Rethinking the development of implicit and explicit memory. *Psychological Review*, **104**, 467–498; and Curran, T. (1997) Effects of aging on implicit sequence learning: Accounting for sequence structure and explicit knowledge. *Psychological Research*, **60**, 24–41.

9. Although recognised in the 19th century, infantile amnesia was not formally demonstrated until Waldfogel, S. (1948) The frequency and affective character of childhood memories. *Psychological Monograph*, **62**, no. 291.

10. From Fivush, R. & Hamond, N.R. (1990) Autobiographical memory across preschool years: Toward reconceptualising childhood amnesia. In R. Fivush & J. Hudson (eds) *Knowing and Remembering in Young Children*. New York: Cambridge University Press.

11. Fivush, R. et al. (1987) Two year olds talk about the past. *Cognitive Development*, **2**, 393–409.

12. Diamond, A. (1990) Rate of maturation of hippocampus and the development of progression of children's performance on the delayed non-matching to sample, and visual paired comparison tasks. In A. Diamond (ed.) *The Development and Neural Bases of Higher Cognitive Functions*, pp. 394–426. New York: New York Academy of Sciences.

13. Bauer, P.J. (1997) Development of memory in early childhood. In N. Cowan (ed.) *The Development of Memory in Childhood*. Hove: Psychology Press.

14. See Baddeley, A.D. (1997) *Human Memory Theory and Practice*, pp. 211–228. Hove: Psychology Press, and Conway, M. (1996) Autobiographical memory. In E.L. Bjork et al. (eds) *Memory. Handbook of Perception and Cognition*. (2nd edn), pp. 165–194.

15. Perner, J. & Ruffman, T. (1995) Episodic memory and autonoetic consciousness: Developmental evidence and a theory of autobiographical amnesia. *Journal of Experimental Child Psychology*, **59**, 516–548.

16. Nelson K. (1993) The psychological and social origins of autobiographical memory. *Psychological Science*, **4**, 7–14.

17. Flavell, J.H. et al. (1966) Spontaneous verbal rehearsal in a memory task as a function of age. *Child Development*, **37**, 283–299. Ornstein, P.A. et al. (1975) Rehearsal processes and children's memory. In P.A. Ornstein (ed.) *Memory Development in Children*. Hillsdale, NJ: Erlbaum. A good recent overview of strategy development in children is given by Bjorklund, D.F. & Douglas, R. (1997) The development of memory strategies. In N. Cowan (ed.) *The Development of Memory in Childhood*. Hove: Psychology Press.

18. Arlin, M. & Brody (1976) Effects of spatial presentation and blocking on organisation and verbal recall at three grade levels. *Developmental Psychology*, **12**, 113–118. Hasselhorn, M. (1990) The emergence of strategic knowledge activation in categorical clustering during retrieval. *Journal of Experimental Child Psychology*, **50**, 59–80. For a recent review of strategy use by children along with other aspects of memory development, see Gathercole, S.E. (1998) The development of memory. *Journal of Child Psychology and Psychiatry and Allied Disciplines*, **39**, 3–27.

19. Kobasigawa, A. (1974) Utilisation of retrieval cues by children in recall. *Child Development*, **45**, 127–134.

20. Guttentag, R. (1997) Memory development and processing resources. In N. Cowan (ed.) *The Development of Memory in Childhood*. Hove: Psychology Press.

21. Farrar, M.J. & Goodman, G.S. (1990) Developmental differences in the relation between scripts and memory: Do they exist? In R. Fivush & J. Hudson (eds) *Knowing and Remembering in Young Children*. New York: Cambridge University Press.

22. Farrar, M.J. & Goodman, G.S. (1992) Developmental changes in event memory. *Child Development*, **63**, 173–187.

23. Bjorklund, D.F. & Schneider, W. (1996) The interaction of knowledge, aptitudes, and strategies in children's memory performance. In H.W. Reese (ed.) *Advances in Child Development and Behaviour*, vol. XXV. San Diego: Academic Press.

24. Kreutzer, M.A. et al. (1975) An interview study of children's knowledge about memory. *Monographs of the Society for Research in Child Development*, **40**, (1, serial no. 159), 1–58.

25. Howard, D.V. et al. (1986) Aging and the time course of activation. *Journal of Gerontology*, **41**, 195–203.
26. For an overall account of age differences in memory see Kausler, D.H. (1994) *Learning and Memory in Normal Aging*. San Diego CA: Academic Press. For a briefer review see Cohen, G. (1996) Memory and learning in normal aging. In R.T. Woods (ed.) *Handbook of the Clinical Psychology of Aging*, pp. 45–58. Chichester: Wiley. Parkin, A.J. (1997) *Memory and Amnesia: An Introduction* (2nd edn), Chapter 7.
27. Bartlett, J.C. & Fulton, A. (1991) Familiarity and recognition of faces. *Memory & Cognition*, **9**, 229–238.
28. Parkin, A.J. & Walter, B.M. (1992) Recollective experience, normal aging, and frontal dysfunction. *Psychology and Aging*, **7**, 290–298.
29. Light, L.L. & Singh, A. (1987) Implicit and explicit memory in young and older adults. *Journal of Experimental Psychology: Learning, Memory & Cognition*, **13**, 531–541.
30. Parkin, A.J. & Russo, R. (1993) Age differences in implicit memory: More apparent than real. *Memory & Cognition*, **21**, 73–80.
31. Cockburn, J. & Smith P.T. (1993) Correlates of everyday memory among residents of Part III homes. *British Journal of Clinical Psychology*, **32**, 75–77. Winocur, G. (1982) *Learning and Memory Deficits in Institutionalised and Non-institutionalised Adults: An Analysis of Interference Effects*. New York: Plenum.
32. Flood, D.G. & Coleman, P.D. (1988) Neuron numbers and sizes in the aging brain: Comparisons of human, monkey, and rodent data. *Neurobiology of Aging*, **9**, 453–463.
33. Hasher, L. & Zacks, R.T. (1988) Working memory comprehension and aging: A review and a new view. In G.H. Bower (ed.) *Psychology of Learning and Motivation*, vol. 22, pp. 193–225. A recent review of the inhibition theory of ageing is provided by McDowd, J.M. (1997) Inhibition in attention and aging. *Journals of Gerontology (Series B), Psychological Sciences and Social Sciences*, **52B**, 265–273.
34. Salthouse has put out a large volume of work supporting the processing speed hypothesis. A useful overview is:

Salthouse, T.A. The processing speed theory of adult age differences in cognition. *Psychological Review*, **103,** 403–428.

35. Parkin, A.J. & Java, R.I. (in press) Determinants of age-related memory loss. In T. Perfect and E.A. Maylor (eds) *Theoretical Debates in Cognitive Aging*. London: Oxford University Press.

4

MEASURING MEMORY

If someone suffers a serious brain injury, he or she will undergo a wide range of assessments. Part of this process will involve some form of assessment to establish the extent to which that person has suffered memory impairment. In this chapter I will describe how a neuropsychologist establishes the extent to which someone has suffered loss of memory.

When someone is first referred for neuropsychological assessment of memory, he or she will have already undergone some degree of neurological examination. Neurologists are concerned with the "hard signs" of brain injury, such as the effects an injury might have on a patient's reflexes, movements, and muscle tone. They may also have carried out some form of **neuroradiological** investigation of the patient's brain injury.[1] In practice, a patient is likely to have had either a **CAT** scan or an **MRI** scan. CAT stands for **computerised axial tomography** and is an X-ray procedure that enables a three-dimensional image of the brain to be set up. In a CAT scan damaged areas of the brain show up as darker areas (see Figure 4.1). MRI (**magnetic resonance imaging**) is a more recent technique which allows a more detailed structural picture of the brain to be derived (see Figure 4.2). With MRI damaged areas can be either darker or lighter depending on the exact method used. MRI is preferred because it can often reveal deficits that were not detectable by CAT scan—indeed the lesion revealed by MRI data in Figure 4.2 went undetected by CAT.

CAT and MRI both provide evidence of structural damage to the brain but the brain can also exhibit **metabolic dysfunction**. Some brain diseases, for example, result in reduced activity (**hypometabolism**) in certain parts of the brain. In these situations the brain tissue is not damaged and is thus not shown as abnormal by CAT or MRI. However, a different form of scan, known as **positron emission tomography**, can reveal metabolic impairments. PET works by measuring the degree of glucose uptake in different parts of the brain. When an area exhibits hypometabolism its energy demands are less and thus its glucose activity is reduced (see Figure 4.3). There is also a less sophisticated version of PET known as **single photon emission computerised tomography** (SPECT) and MRI has been adapted to measure metabolic changes—this is known as **functional magnetic resonance imaging** (fMRI).

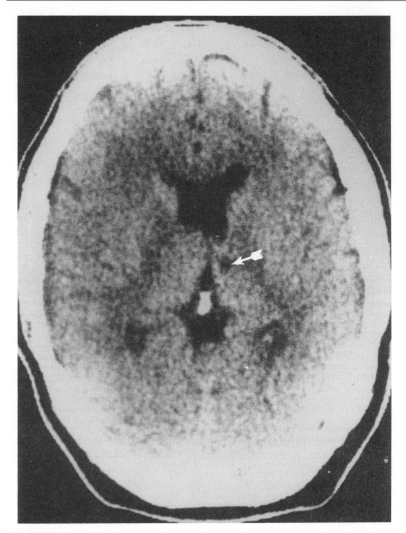

Figure 4.1: An image of the brain produced by computerised axial tomography (CAT). Most of the dark areas represent the ventricles of the brain which are filled with cerebro-spinal fluid. However, the small dark area indicated is the site of a small stroke in the thalamus. As a result of the stroke the cells have died and the fluid has filled the space. Although small, this lesion, occurring where it did, caused a severe amnesia. (From Speedie, L.J. & Heliman, K.M. (1982) Amnesic disturbance following infarction of the left dorsomedial nucleus of the thalamus. *Neuropsychologia*, **20**, 579–604.)

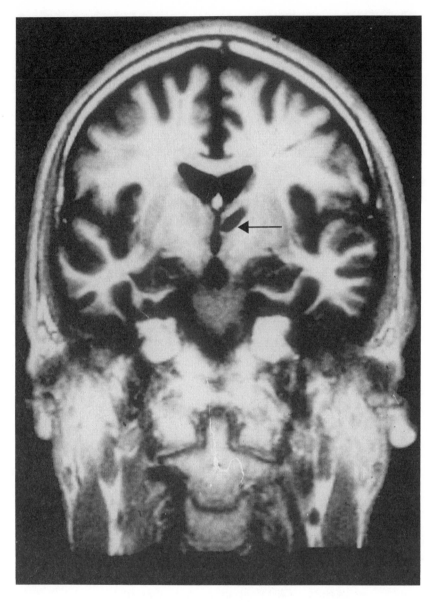

Figure 4.2: An image of the brain produced by magnetic resonance imaging (MRI). This again shows the results of a small stroke in the thalamus, indicated by arrow. Note the much greater definition achieved by MRI.

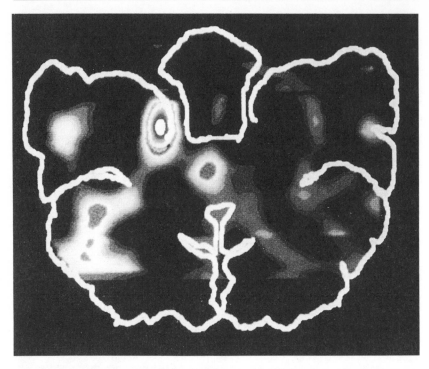

Figure 4.3: An image of the brain produced positron emission tomography (PET). Brighter areas indicate greater brain activity. This
image would usually be in colour. (Photograph courtesy of Larry
Squire.)

NEUROPSYCHOLOGICAL ASSESSMENT OF MEMORY

As we have seen in previous chapters, memory is not a single
entity like height so there is no single measure we can take to
establish the extent of impairment. Instead the clinician needs to
take a variety of measurements based on tests that tap different
forms of memory. The first issue about a memory assessment is
when it should be taken. Most brain insults produce a pattern of

impairments that is far more severe in the early stages of recovery than at a later stage. For this reason I believe that detailed assessments carried out immediately post-injury are of little value in predicting—and thus are of little use in making judgements about—long-term outcome. In the case of head injury, the most frequent basis of claims for brain injury, I believe that an assessment carried out about one-year post-injury is going to provide an accurate picture of a person's lasting memory impairment. Many lawyers reading this book will be aware that settlements for damages arising from brain damage often take several years to occur. The excuse for this enormous delay is that the proper extent of a brain injury can only be established after this kind of period. There is, in my opinion, no scientific or medical basis supporting this view and that the interminable delays victims of head injury face are entirely unjustified. Similarly, an accurate picture of memory loss can also be established quite soon following most other causes of memory impairment (i.e. between 6 and 9 months). The only exception to this appears to be ruptured aneurysms of the anterior communicating artery (see p. 94) where, for some reason, significant recovery of memory can occur after considerably longer delays.

THE MEMORY "BATTERY"

As the name implies, a memory battery involves a number of tests. However, unlike an artillery battery where all the guns are similar, each component of the memory battery is aimed at testing a different memory function. The battery I prefer to use is the **Wechsler Memory Scale—Revised** (WMS-R).[2] The WMS-R is an American test but it exists in a UK form (as well as other languages) and is widely used. It comprises nine tests which are divided into two basic kinds, verbal and visual. The verbal tests assess mental control (e.g. reciting the alphabet), logical memory (memory for a story), learning of verbal associations and memory span (digit span). The visual tests comprise learning of visual associations, memory for abstract designs, figural memory, and visual memory span.

When a client has completed all these tests the scores can be combined in different ways to obtain **memory indices**. In all, five indices can be derived from WMS-R: verbal memory, visual memory, general memory, attention/concentration, and delayed memory. The WMS-R has been administered to a large number of individuals and this has enabled **normative data** about the test to be produced. As the name suggests, normative data give information about how the population as a whole perform on the tests. Using these data, indices have been constructed so that they have an average of 100 and a standard deviation of 15. Standard deviation is a statistical term which refers to the distribution of scores around an average. On the assumption that memory abilities are natural phenomena like height and weight, we can assume that 66% of the population will have a score within one standard deviation of the average and that 99% of the population would be plus or minus two standard deviations from the average. Thus, in the case of WMS-R indices, 66% of the population would score between 85 and 115 on any given index and 99% between 70 and 130.

Armed with these indices the clinician can now make some judgement about whether a person's memory is impaired or not. A score of 100 is obviously average; 85–99 below average; and 101–115 above average. Scores falling more than two standard deviations below the mean (i.e. 69 or less) are clearly indicative of memory impairment whereas scores above 130 represent exceptionally good memory. In practice an index of below 80 is usually considered evidence of impairment. Thus, WMS-R manual shows that head-injured patients around 27 years old have a general memory index of 77. Other disorders of memory typically produce much lower indices. Korsakoff's syndrome (see p. 92), for example, has an average general memory index of 67 and those with Alzheimer's disease manage only 62.

The WMS-R has one additional feature which also helps in the diagnosis of memory impairment. If we give a memory test, or indeed any other kind of test, to a large sample of people we will get a variation in scores. Providing the sample population is big enough to be representative we can describe these variations in terms of **percentile ranks**. A percentile rank is a statistical means which enables you to determine the percentage of people scoring at or below a given level in the general population. For example, a person may score 8/20 on a test. Examination of the scores from the sample indicates that 15% of the population score at or below this level, indicating that the person is well below average on that test. In the WMS-R percentiles are available for memory span, logical memory and figural memory and these can be useful in providing more information about the nature of memory loss. In particular, the percentiles for logical memory and figural memory can be helpful in interpreting the verbal and visual memory indices. Both of these indices contain, as one component, the client's score on memory span. In my opinion there is a problem with this because memory span taps a different form of memory to that involved in the other subtests of verbal or visual memory. In a previous chapter we saw that memory is divided into short-term and long-term storage systems. By their very nature the WMS-R span tasks assess STS function whereas the other subtests rely on LTS function. Moreover, as we shall see in a later chapter, STS function can often be preserved in cases of severe memory loss. As a result combining span performance with other memory tests could inflate a client's score and cover up a memory disorder. There are fortunately two ways around this problem. First, the delayed memory index does not consider span performance. However, if this is not available, the percentiles for logical and figural memory should give a more accurate assessment of memory.

OTHER ASSESSMENTS OF MEMORY

In a perfect world there would be only one standard memory assessment which everyone would use. While the WMS-R is the most widely used, and the one for which there is the most statistical data, there are numerous other tests in circulation.[3] The reason other tests are used is varied. The original WMS was shunned by many because it did not contain tests of visual or delayed memory. This is no longer the case but others object to it on the grounds that it takes too long to administer and that parts of it are stressful for someone with a poor memory. One response to this has been the development of **screening tests** which provide a simpler and quicker assessment of memory which, in addition, does not require a psychologist to administer it or interpret the results.

The most widely used screening test is the **Rivermead Behavioural Memory Test** (RBMT) which is also one of the few memory tests to have a version for children.[4] One aim of the test is "face validity"—the idea that the memory measures used actually reflect real-life memory tasks. Thus the test examines memory for a name, memory for a hidden belonging, and remembering a route. This test produces a screening score classifying the client's memory as either severely impaired, moderately impaired, poor, or normal. While this test is of great value in providing evidence that someone has a severe to moderate memory deficit, it is far less sensitive to more subtle impairments of memory such as those arising from mild head injury, i.e. many people with significant memory loss pass the RBMT. Failure on RBMT is evidence of marked memory loss but passing the test is not evidence of normal memory and further investigation must be carried out.

Test sensitivity is also an issue with another widely used test, the **Recognition Memory Test** (RMT).[5] This test involves showing people a sequence of words or faces and giving them a recognition test in which pairs of items are presented and the individuals must decide which of those two items was the one previously seen. Again, failure on this test is indicative of memory loss but good performance does not necessarily mean good memory. A patient I saw recently, for example, scored 48/50 on recognition of words (90th percentile) but his logical memory was at the 5th percentile! In this case conclusions based just on the RMT are misleading.

Within the scope of this book it is impossible to review all the memory tests used by clinicians. I can only offer some guidelines about what to do if confronted with assessment information about a client. First you need to know whether the scores obtained by the client can be related to a standardisation sample. If this is not the case then the client's score on the tests is uninterpretable because you do not know what constitutes normal performance. You also need to know whether the sample is stratified for age, i.e. that the normal scores given reflect natural changes with age. You also need to know whether the test that has been given is sensitive to deficits. A test that is far too easy, or tests a component of memory that is usually spared in memory disorder, is useless as a basis for saying that someone's memory is normal.

WHEN IS A PERSON "AMNESIC"

There are a number of situations in which someone may wish to claim that he or she is "amnesic"—i.e. suffering disabling memory loss. Unfortunately, amnesia is a relative term and cannot be used in the same way as disease labels such as chickenpox and measles. To understand this we have to return to the WMS-R.

An important constraint in the interpretation of WMS-R scores concerns a person's **intelligence quotient** (IQ). An IQ is typically derived from another of Wechsler's tests, the **Wechsler Adult Intelligence Scale—Revised** (WAIS-R).[2] The WAIS-R produces three indices, a verbal IQ, a performance IQ, and a full-scale IQ—the latter being derived from the other two. Like the WMS-R indices, the WAIS-R indices have a mean of 100 and a standard deviation of 15. The verbal subtests involve such things as defining words and comprehension ability whereas the performance subtests largely assess visually-based abilities. IQ and memory are strongly related as good performance on IQ measures predicts an above-average memory. As a result, a person's IQ must be taken into account when assessing a person's memory deficit. Consider two people scoring 100 on the general memory index of WMS-R. One of them has a full-scale IQ of 105 while the other has an IQ of 130. In the first case we would not suspect memory impairment but in the second we would, simply because someone with that level of IQ should score a lot better than 100.

As for the presence of "amnesia" many clinicians would consider a memory index between 20 and 25 points lower than IQ as indicative of significant memory impairment. However, to call every instance of this "amnesia" is difficult because, for example, a person with an IQ of 130 and a memory index of 107 still has an above-average memory! Clinically I think it is much clearer to talk about degrees of memory impairment in relation to intellectual status rather than pursue a clinical definition of amnesia. For me the term "amnesia" is best used to describe a pattern of impairment in which memory is affected disproportionately to intellect rather than to imply an individual who has completely lost his or her memory.

MEMORY FOR THE PAST

Clinical assessments of memory concentrate on an individuals' ability to remember new information. A problem in acquiring new knowledge is a defining feature of memory disorder and is known as **anterograde amnesia**. However, people with memory disorder also have problems remembering information that was acquired before the injury or illness that brought on loss of memory—this period of time is known as the **pre-morbid period** and contrasts with the **post-morbid period** of memory difficulty reflected in anterograde amnesia. Loss of memory for the pre-morbid period is known as **retrograde amnesia** and this can be present in varying degrees in people suffering from anterograde amnesia. It is important to note that the severity of retrograde amnesia may not be related to the severity of anterograde amnesia.

Assessing retrograde amnesia is problematic because each person's past experience is different so there is no way of knowing what a particular individual should be able to remember about his or her past. Thus asking an individual about world events may be misleading if that person took no interest in such things. Despite this, one test has been devised to provide a standardised assessment of pre-morbid memory. The **Autobiographical Memory Interview** (AMI)[6] assesses two aspects of memory, personal semantic and autobiographic. In Chapter 2 we saw that there is a tendency to think of memory as either episodic or semantic. Episodic memory is memory for personal events and corresponds directly to what is meant by autobiographical memory. Personal semantic memory relates to the idea that we have general knowledge about ourselves as well as other things in the world. Thus we know that we got married in 1984 without having to remember the specific experience.

The AMI is divided into three sections: childhood, early adult life, and recent life. A series of personal semantic questions are asked about each time period (e.g. What primary school did you go to?, Where did you get married?) along with an autobiographical assessment. The latter requires the person to remember a specific incident from his or her life (e.g. an incident involving you and a friend at school). Two scores are derived, one for each form of memory, and sample data enable an impairment to be identified. Memory-impaired patients tend to produce a particular pattern of performance on the test. First, they will generally do better on questions relating to earlier parts of their lives. This is a very reliable finding and reflects something known as **Ribot's law** which states that the vulnerability of a memory to brain injury is inversely proportional to its age—the older a memory the more likely it is to survive a brain insult. The second finding is that patients will tend to perform more poorly on the autobiographical component.

I have found the AMI useful as a means of assessing pre-morbid memory and a useful way of obtaining more general information about a client's background. However, there are a number of problems. Establishing the truth of a client's memory in the absence of a relative or friend to confirm it is an obvious difficulty. Also, with only three time periods, the transition between pre- and post-morbid period will fall within one section.

In addition, the test assumes the modal arrangement of marriage, children, and assumes that the client is hospitalised. The alternative questions for people who do not meet these criteria are somewhat more difficult.

IS A MEMORY DISORDER GENUINE?

Very often proof of memory impairment forms part of the basis for claiming damages or can provide mitigating circumstances in the case of prosecution. This immediately raises the issue that someone might attempt to exaggerate or completely fake loss of memory for personal gain—typically known as **malingering**. In the case of people claiming damages for the effects of head injury the exaggeration of memory problems is so well known that it has even been given a name—**compensation neurosis**—thus clients with apparently disabling memory impairments make a remarkable "recovery" once their compensation payment has been settled. In terms of assessment this means that an individual might deliberately underachieve on memory tests in order to give the impression of impaired memory.[7] How then can the psychologist be sure that a memory deficit is genuine?

In order to assess whether a memory impairment is genuine the psychologist must first seek a motive for possible exaggeration. Most people simulating a memory disorder do so for a reason. This may be financial, as in the case of compensation claims, a means of avoiding prosecution, or attention-seeking behaviour brought on by adverse personal circumstances. It is very unusual to discover simulated memory impairments in the absence of some obvious motive. Another suspicious circumstance is the absence of any identifiable brain injury or any event that could have caused such an injury. However, one has to be careful here. First, many patients undergo only routine examination following a head injury. As we saw above, patients will be referred for neuropsychological assessment with varying degrees of neuroradiological information which, in turn, vary in their sensitivity to the presence of brain damage. Some will have no scan information, some will have CAT scan data, and others MRI. In addition, even a clean MRI does not mean that damage is not present and there is always the possibility of a metabolic disorder which could only be detected by PET. Within this context one can only be strongly suspicious if the predisposing events are unlikely to have caused any damage, e.g. an injury that did not cause loss of consciousness, and there is also no evidence of brain injury.

However, even when a brain injury is present there can still be elements of simulation that need to be considered. In a recent case a man was found in Glasgow suffering from amnesia and unable to explain how he got there. It transpired that he was awaiting trial for fraud. While the psychologists found obvious elements of simulation in his behaviour he was also found to have a brain lesion that could have affected his memory.[8]

While lack of brain injury and motive may be sufficient to conclude that someone is simulating a memory disorder, it is also necessary to carry out a memory assessment. The basis of this assessment is that someone simulating a memory disorder does not actually know what a memory disorder is like. In particular, the person may not realise that someone with a memory impairment does not normally fail all memory tests. A good example of this is the WMS-R. Earlier we noted that memory span is most often preserved in people with even severe memory disorder despite poor performance on other subtests, i.e. these people still manage a span of 7 plus or minus 2. Failure on memory span should thus be viewed as suspicious. Another approach involves the use of memory tests that are presented as apparently difficult when in fact they are easy. A test of this kind is shown in Figure 4.4. The person is told that 15 items will be shown for only 10 seconds—the implication being that the test is difficult when, in fact, even people with quite marked memory loss can do quite well. In using this test it is generally thought that failure to remember less than three lines is evidence of simulation.[9]

Simulators "get it wrong" in other ways. We also saw above that personal semantic memory, especially for the earlier parts of life, tends to be preserved. Studies have now shown that

Figure 4.4: The malingering test produced by Rey, A. (1964) *L'examen clinique en psychologie.* Paris: Presses Universitaires de France.

people attempting simulation do not know this and wrongly fail to remember early events about their lives. It has also been shown that simulators contrive to perform **below chance** on recognition tests. In one investigation a man on trial for murdering his wife claimed that he had amnesia. He was given a recognition test rather like the Recognition Memory Test (see above) and produced a score of well below 50% correct—something that would only be possible if you knew which answer was correct and deliberately chose the other one.

In sum, psychologists have a variety of means of detecting a simulated memory disorder but it is usually the case that several lines of evidence need to point to the same conclusion before one can be absolutely certain that memory loss is not genuine. Moreover, one should also be careful about considering a simulator as fake in the absolute sense. What the assessment tells you is that the memory disorder is not genuine in the sense that it could not arise from a brain injury. It does not follow that the person is therefore "normal"—persistence with a simulated memory disorder can often be a psychopathological sign that warrants further investigation.

SUMMARY

- Structural images of the brain can be produced by CAT or MRI.

- In order to detect metabolic disturbance in the brain the technique of PET must be used. More recently the same has been achieved with SPECT and fMRI.
- Memory assessment is most accurate when the acute effects of brain injury have disappeared.
- Because memory is a multi-component process, it is best assessed via a battery of memory tests.
- The most commonly used memory test is the Wechsler Memory Scale, but this may not always be sufficient.
- For a memory test to be useful it must be standardised.
- Amnesia is best defined in terms of a person's memory relative to an assessment of his or her intelligence.
- Impaired memory for new information is known as anterograde amnesia. Impaired memory for pre-injury/illness information is known as retrograde amnesia.
- There are far more tests for anterograde than for retrograde amnesia. The AMI is one of the few standardised tests of retrograde amnesia.
- Memory disorders may not always be genuine and can be detected using tests which exploit the fact that simulators do not fully understand the nature of amnesia.

NOTES AND REFERENCES

1. For a good introduction to neuroimaging see Posner, M.I. & Raichle, M.E. (1994) *Images of Mind*. New York: Freeman.
2. Wechsler, D. (1987) *Wechsler Memory Scale—Revised*. New York: Psychological Corporation. At the time of writing a new version of the WMS has been released. This new test, *WMS 3rd Edition*, incorporates some of the WMS-R tests plus a range of new tests. It has been developed to be used in conjunction with Wechsler Adult Intelligence Scale (WAIS-III). WMS-R, 3rd edition, has just been released in the UK. WAIS-III is currently unavailable in English format so the WAIS-R is the one commonly used: Wechsler, D. (1984)

Wechsler Adult Intelligence Scale—Revised. New York: Psychologial Corporation.

3. There are many sources for finding out more about memory tests. The most comprehensive is Lezak, M.D. (1995) *Neuropsychological Assessment* (3rd edn). New York: Oxford University Press. See also Mayes, A. & Warburg, R. (1992) *Memory Assessment in Clinical Practice and Research*. In J.R. Crawford et al. (eds) *A Handbook of Neuropsychological Assessment*. Hove: Erlbaum. A recent book of my own also covers memory assessment: Parkin, A.J. (1997) *Memory & Amnesia: An Introduction* (2nd edn). Oxford: Basil Blackwell. See also Kramer, J.H. & Delis, D.C. (1998) Neuropsychological assessment of memory. In G. Goldstein et al. (eds) *Neuropsychology of Human Brain Function: Assessment and Rehabilitation*, pp. 333–356. New York: Plenum.

4. Wilson, B.A., Cockburn, J. & Baddeley, A.D. (1985) *The Rivermead Behavioural Memory Test*. Bury St Edmunds: Thames Valley Test Co; Wilson, B.A., Ivani-Chalian, R. & Aldrich, F.K. (1991) *The Rivermead Behavioural Memory Test for Children Aged 5–10 years*. Bury St Edmunds: Thames Valley Test Co.

5. Warrington, E.K. (1984) *Recognition Memory Test*. London: NFER: Nelson.

6. Kopelman, M.D., Wilson, B.A. & Baddeley, A.D. (1990) *The Autobiographical Memory Interview*. Bury St Edmunds: Thames Valley Test Co.

7. Compensation neurosis is a controversial topic, particularly in terms of its frequency within litigants and its causality: Mendelson, G. (1995) Compensation neurosis revisited. Outcome studies of the effects of litigation. *Journal of Psychosomatic Research*, **39**, 695–706. See also: Mayou, R. (1997) Accident neurosis revisited. *British Journal of Psychiatry*, **168**, 399–403. Reynolds, C.R. (ed.) (1998) *Detection of Malingering during Head Injury Litigation: Critical Issues in Clinical Neuropsychology*. New York: Plenum.

8. Kopelman, M.D. (1995) The case of the amnesic intelligence officer. *Psychological Medicine*, **24**, 1037–1045.

9. A recent review of methods for detecting malingering can be found in Leng, N.R.C. & Parkin, A.J. (1995) The detection of

exaggerated or simulated memory disorder by neuropsychological methods. *Journal of Psychosomatic Research*, **39**, 767–776. See also Rogers, R. et al. *Clinical Assessment of Malingering and Deception* (2nd edn). New York: Guilford. The value of digit span as a test of malingering is shown by Prigatano, G. et al. (1997) Suspected malingering and the digit memory test: A replication and extension. *Archives of Clinical Neuropsychology*, **12**, 609–619. An intriguing case study describing an investigation of malingering is provided by Kopelman, M.D., Puffet, A. & Stanhope, N. (1994) The great escape. *Neuropsychologia*, **32**, 675–691.

5

THE CAUSES OF
MEMORY LOSS

The aim of this chapter is to cover the major causes of memory loss. All causes of memory loss lead to two forms of deficit: an **anterograde** deficit (e.g. the name of the doctor dealing with you) and **retrograde** deficits (e.g. the name or even the ability to recognise a well-known relative as familiar). Every form of memory impairment involves anterograde deficits[1] but, depending on the cause, the extent of retrograde impairment is variable. Causes of memory impairment are also divisible into those that cause permanent loss of memory and those in which memory loss is temporary.

PERMANENT MEMORY LOSS

There are many causes of permanent memory loss and some of them are very unusual. I once, for example, worked with a man who became amnesic due to radiotherapy for nasal cancer—which is very unusual, particularly in the West.[2] There are also diseases where memory loss features as an issue but where other symptoms are more predominant. These include schizophrenia, Huntington's chorea, Parkinson's disease, AIDS, diabetes, and multiple sclerosis. In writing this chapter I decided to concentrate on those illnesses and injuries in which memory loss is the primary symptom.

Head Injury

Head injury comes in two basic forms: **penetrating** and **closed**. As the name suggests, a penetrating head injury involves an object entering the brain in some way. Pictures of penetrating head injuries often look horrific but the outcome can be surprisingly good. Figure 5.1 shows the skull of a man known as Lewis Avery who lived for many years unaware that part of his musket was embedded in his brain. More recently there have been a number of cases of seemingly dramatic injuries having relatively small effects. Figure 5.2, for example, shows the brain of a man who fired a nail gun up his nose while severely drunk and then forgot about it. Several years later he was admitted while unconscious and a routine scan picked up the nail embedded deep in his brain. There was no evidence that this injury had in any way impaired him.

It would be wrong to say that penetrating head injuries are always relatively harmless—a lot depends on exactly where the penetration occurs. In a much discussed case, a man known as NA was accidentally stabbed up the nose by a fencing foil, the tip of which came to rest in the centre of his brain. Here the effects were dramatic in that the injury caused severe loss of memory. Similar effects were recently reported following an unpleasant incident with a snooker cue.[3]

Closed head injuries are very different to penetrating head injuries in that there is no penetration of the skull by an object—

Figure 5.1: The unusual penetrating head injury suffered by Lewis Avery.

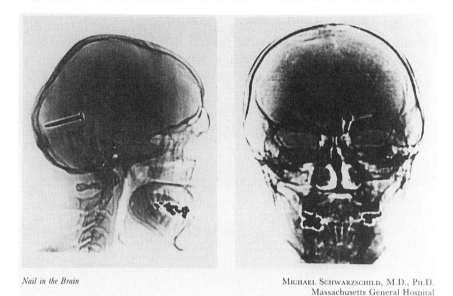

Nail in the Brain

MICHAEL SCHWARZSCHILD, M.D., PH.D.
Massachusetts General Hospital
Boston, MA 02114

Figure 5.2: A nail in the brain. Surprisingly the victim did not know it was there. Like the Lewis Avery case this shows that brain lesions do not always have marked effects. It very much depends on where the damage actually occurs.

although often there will be a fracture. A closed head injury is caused by the head impacting on some hard surface—as might be caused by crashing into a car windscreen or falling to the ground. The often devastating consequences of closed head injury arise from what one might consider a design fault of the human body. The brain is encased by the skull to prevent it from injury. However, it is this encasement that leads to the extensive damage so frequently seen with this kind of injury. Essentially when the head hits a hard surface it stops moving, but inside the head the brain is still moving and, because of its encasement, cannot go forward. Under these conditions the brain can only rotate on its central axis, which results in the shearing of brain tissue as twisting occurs. In addition to this twisting there may be a **contre coup** injury in which the brain is impacted against the part of the skull opposite the site of the injury.

The effects of closed head injury are often widespread although, for certain mechanical reasons, they tend to be predominantly in the temporal and frontal lobes. As we saw in Chapter 1, these areas are critical to memory function so it is no surprise that loss of memory is the commonest outcome of closed head injury. Immediately following a closed head injury a patient may be unconscious for some time and the duration of **coma** is a reasonable predictor of outcome: longer periods of coma predict poorer outcome. After that there is a period known as **post-traumatic amnesia (PTA)** during which the patient exhibits severe memory problems and is also confused and disoriented. PTA lasts a variable amount of time, after which some recovery will be noted and the full extent of the patient's permanent impairments will be apparent.[4]

Encephalitis

There are many forms of encephalitis (pl. encephalitides), but there is insufficient space to describe all of them here. By far the most severe, in terms of memory loss, is **herpes simplex encephalitis (HSE)**. This is the same virus that causes mouth ulcers, cold sores and genital herpes. Viruses are never lost from the body, they remain dormant and suddenly have effects particularly under stress. Many of you know how mouth ulcers can erupt under times of stress. For reasons that are still unknown the herpes simplex virus can sometimes become neuropathogenic, i.e. it attacks brain tissue. Fortunately this is very rare, but for the individuals concerned the effects are devastating. Encephalitis literally means inflammation of the brain and victims of encephalitis suffer because their symptoms are of a **protean** nature in that their problems resemble the characteristics of other less harmful diseases like influenza. For this reason the disease can go undetected for days or even weeks while the patient is treated for the lesser ailment. This delay is crucial because the herpes simplex virus can cause severe and irreversible brain damage within 24 hours.

At one time HSE was fatal, but it can now be treated by the drug *Zovirax* which you may have seen on sale as a treatment for cold sores. The drug is very effective but is rarely administered quickly enough to prevent the onset of significant brain damage. Again, for reasons that are unknown the virus has a predilection for attacking the temporal lobes of the brain and for this reason causes a dense amnesia (see Figure 5.3). People who have survived HSE will almost invariably have a moderate to severe anterograde amnesia and the extent of retrograde amnesia can often be extensive. Other symptoms may also be present if the disease process has sufficiently advanced. These symptoms include hypersexuality and hyperphagia—the latter being a tendency to eat anything. (I very much remember one HSE patient who could not resist eating telephone directories—something that was very distressing for his relatives.) The prognosis for HSE is poor and the extent of the symptoms that are present six months after infection is likely to represent the permanent state of affairs.[5]

Varicella zoster is the virus that causes chickenpox and can, later in life, reappear and cause encephalitis (see Figure 5.3(a)). Herpes zoster encephalitis has been studied far less, but from what we know its effect on memory is less devastating than herpes simplex. Arthropod-borne viruses, or "arboviruses", are also an important cause of encephalitis world wide, although not in UK because the vector of these illnesses is a different species of mosquito. Four arbovirus encephalitides have been identified: St Louis encephalitis, Western equine encephalitis, Eastern equine encephalitis, and California encephalitis. All four can give rise to permanent neurological damage, including loss of memory. There is also a form of encephalitis carried by bats and a range of other agents that can cause encephalitic illness.

Alcohol and Memory

Many of us have experienced hazy memory as a result of too much to drink, and this can have important implications in legal settings in that a person might be unable to give evidence as a

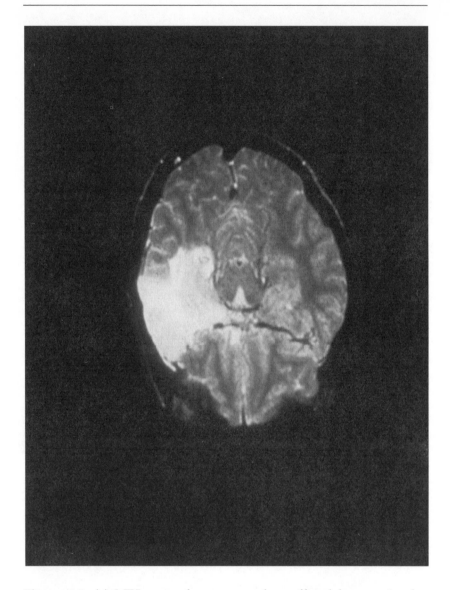

Figure 5.3: (a) MRI scan of someone who suffered herpes simplex encephalitis. The large blank area on the left represents the area destroyed by the virus. (b) (opposite) MRI scan of a patient following brain infection with herpes varicella zoster—note the large blank region on the right.

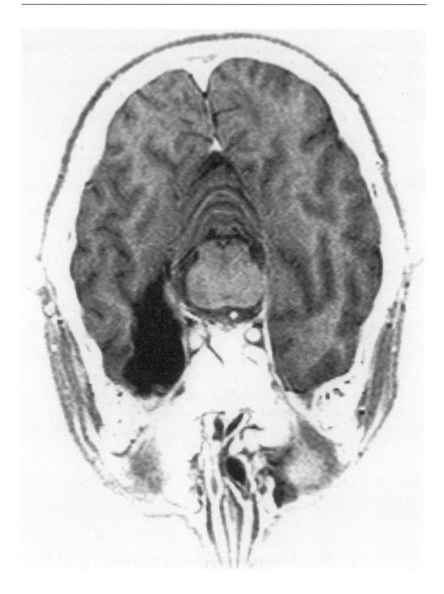

consequence of intoxication. It is impossible to set specific guidelines as to how much alcohol is needed to impair memory significantly because the same amount of alcohol can affect people's memory differently. Thus a hardened drinker might have good recall after six pints, whereas an inexperienced drinker might remember next to nothing. It is thus a matter of judgement as to whether the evidence of an intoxicated person should be believed.[6]

Alcohol causes the brain to dehydrate and thus shrink, but this effect reverses if abstinence is observed. However, there are circumstances in which prolonged alcohol abuse can cause permanent brain damage, producing a condition known as **Korsakoff's syndrome**. It is often mistakenly thought that this disease arises from the direct effects of alcohol on the brain, but this is incorrect. The actual cause is that prolonged exposure to alcohol leads to a deficiency in the absorption of a vitamin known as thiamine which, in turn, leads to haemorrhaging in certain parts of the brain, particularly in the diencephalon (see Figure 5.4). Korsakoff's syndrome is more likely to occur if an alcoholic ceases to eat, but there is also evidence of a genetic disposition towards the illness. Thus some people are able to consume vast amounts of alcohol and not develop the disorder, whereas others can be afflicted from a similar alcohol intake.

The onset of Korsakoff's syndrome is signalled by the appearance of **Wernicke's disease**. This typically involves three symptoms: confusion, staggering gait, and poor control of eye movements. The latter two disappear leaving the patient with a profound and permanent memory disorder which involves a severe anterograde amnesia and usually a severe retrograde amnesia as well. Thus a Korsakoff patient, when asked the price of something, might suggest a price that is 20 or even 30 years out of date. Once Korsakoff's syndrome has set in, there is little improvement.

Strokes and Aneurysms

To function normally the brain needs a constant supply of blood. If for some reason the supply to the brain is disrupted the brain cells in those affected areas very quickly die. There are two common forms of disruption. In a **stroke** or **cerebrovascular accident (CVA)** an artery becomes blocked either due to a blood

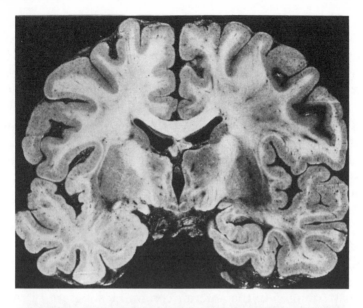

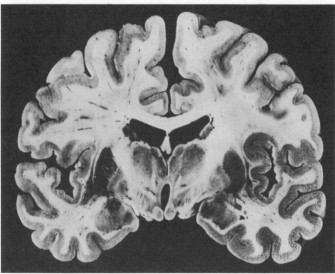

Figure 5.4: Brain of someone who suffered from Korsakoff's syndrome (top) compared with a similar section of a normal brain (bottom). Note the large area of damage at the bottom of the brain which has completely destroyed the mamillary bodies.

clot or through thickening due to disease. The effect of a stroke is to cut off the blood supply to a part of the brain and the resulting deficit will depend on which part of the brain is affected. If a stroke affects either the temporal lobe region or the diencephalon there is a strong possibility that loss of memory will occur. However, strokes can often be very specific in the areas they affect so that strokes in these regions may not always affect memory. The effect that strokes have on memory can be variable. Sometimes they just affect the acquisition of new memories but they can additionally affect remote memories.

An aneurysm is effectively a bulge in an artery caused by weakening of the arterial wall. In some cases aneurysm rupture and an emergency operation is needed to repair the damaged blood vessel. It is in these circumstances that aneurysms most readily lead to brain damage. While aneurysms can occur in many parts of the brain's arterial circulation they are particularly common in the anterior communicating artery (ACoA: see Figure 5.3(b)). This is a small artery connecting the two anterior cerebral arteries but rupture of the ACoA can have devastating effects on memory. These effects are, however, somewhat different to those we see in other permanent disorders such as encephalitis and Korsakoff's syndrome[7]. Very often these patients appear to have a less severe disorder of memory, being quite good at recognition despite poor recall, and this is because the aneurysm does not affect the temporal lobe or diencephalon but instead damages structures associated with the frontal lobes.[8]

Dementia

With the rise in physical health we are now becoming all too aware of dementia, particularly in the increasing number of people who live beyond 80. Dementia is not just a loss of memory, it is an all-round deterioration of mental abilities; however, loss of memory is often its first and most prominent sign. Thus the demented person starts to ask the same questions repeatedly and become confused in time and place. Unlike most other forms of memory loss there is also a deterioration in memory span. Later in the illness problems with language arise, followed by difficulties dressing and eating. The commonest cause of dementia is **Alzheimer's disease** in which the brain is characterised by numerous plaques and neurofibrally tangles in the brain cells. The second most common cause of dementia is **vascular** or **multi-infarct dementia** (**MID**). As the name implies, this form of dementia is caused by deterioration in the blood supply to the person's brain and, in effect, takes the form of a series of "mini-strokes" each of which gradually worsens the person's mental condition. MID is thus distinguishable from Alzheimer's disease because it involves a series of discrete stages whereas the decline in the latter is far more gradual.[9] There are also many other rarer forms of dementia such as **Pick's disease** and a group of dementias known collectively as **panencephalopathies**, the most well known of which is **bovine spongiform encephalopathy** (**BSE**)—an illness that has been linked to an infectious agent in beef.

Because of the prevalence of Alzheimer's disease there has been a great deal of interest in finding drugs that can either halt or reverse the disorder. A drug has now been licensed for the treatment of Alzheimer's disease, *Aricept*, but its effects are modest and the development of an effective treatment for this debilitating condition seems a long way off.

TEMPORARY CAUSES OF MEMORY LOSS

Electroconvulsive therapy (ECT)

There are few medical treatments more controversial than ECT. Thought originally to have been derived from the Roman habit of wrapping electric eels around the heads of the mentally disturbed, the treatment involves the placement of electrodes on the scalp and the passing of an electric current through the brain with the aim of causing a seizure. Commonly an electrode is placed in the temporal lobe region on each side of the head although sometimes, in an effort to reduce after-effects, both electrodes are placed on the same side of the head. ECT is delivered under anaesthetic so the patient cannot remember the treatment, but there is also a period of amnesia after the treatment which can vary depending on the type of ECT given. Memory loss is not surprising given placement of electrodes in the temporal lobe regions which, as we have seen, are crucial for memory.

There are two controversies surrounding ECT. First, there is the issue of whether it is of help to patients with certain mental illness. There is debate here but some agreement that it helps patients with a depression that does not respond to drugs. The second issue is whether ECT damages the brain. There are a number of popular books (e.g. *ECT is Bad for Your Brain*) which make anecdotal claims that ECT does cause permanent brain injury. However, controlled studies tell a very different picture and present no evidence of long-term harmful effects following the treatment. It is thought that many claims of brain damage following ECT are from patients who are still on medication that is causing memory disturbance, or from patients who have always had bad memories but did not focus on this until they had been treated. Nonetheless, even proponents of ECT accept that a small percentage of people may be susceptible to long-term harmful effects from the treatment.[10]

Transient Global Amnesia (TGA)

TGA is a somewhat unusual disorder in which an otherwise healthy person suddenly develops a severe loss of memory. A typical patient will ask repeated questions about where he or she is, and immediately forget the answer. There will also be a degree of retrograde amnesia which may vary from a few hours to many years. An attack of TGA typically lasts between 4 and 12 hours. Interestingly, as the memory impairment resolves, the retrograde loss shows a "shrinking" effect with memories from the more remote past returning before those of the more recent past.

TGA can be precipitated by stress, including sexual inter-course, emotional events, strenuous exertion and adverse life events. The physiological cause is still debated but one clue comes from the above-average association of TGA and migraine. This has led to the idea that, for some reason, there is a depression of activity in the hippocampal region of the brain which interferes with both the formation of new memories and the retrieval of pre-existing memories.[11]

Transient Epileptic Amnesia (TEA)

There can be occasions when an epileptic seizure produces a memory disorder that seems remarkably like TGA. However, analysis shows that the disorder is somewhat different. TEA patients tend to be older and the episodes are briefer than TGA. Also unlike TGA, the disorder is recurrent whereas TGA is usu-ally experienced only once. As in TGA there is repetitive ques-tioning and there may be a variable retrograde amnesia. However, the anterograde amnesia may be less severe. Two-thirds of patients with TEA have other forms of epileptic seizure but for about one-third TEA is the only indication that they have epilepsy.[12]

Drugs and Memory

If you remember the 1960s you weren't there—or so the saying goes. However, does the use of marijuana impair memory? There is plenty of anecdotal evidence that marijuana intoxication impairs memory and this is borne out by early experimental evidence. One study examined the influence of marijuana on the free recall task (see Chapter 1). The drug had no influence on the size of the recency effect but lowered performance on earlier parts of the list, thus suggesting a selective impairment of LTS.[13] Other studies have examined whether marijuana affects the storage or retrieval of memories. In one case subjects studied lists before and while smoking marijuana. Only the recall of those lists studied while smoking marijuana was impaired, thus indicating that the drug only affected storage[14]—however, note also that marijuana does cause state-dependent learning in some circumstances (see Chapter 2), indicating that its effects are not solely restricted to storage.

The **benzodiazepines** are a widely used class of drugs commonly associated with memory problems. Most benzodiazepines, such as diazepam (valium) and lorazepam (ativan), can be used either to induce sleep at night (hypnotics) or to reduce anxiety (anxiolytics). With overnight use these drugs can impair memory to a small extent[15] but taken as anxiolytics their effect on memory can be far more obvious. Taken intravenously, benzodiazepines can have marked effects on an individual's ability to learn new information but, as with marijuana, the drug does not affect information learned immediately before drug administration—once again indicating that the drug interferes with consolidation.[16] In some instances the amnesia produced by benzodiazepines can be advantageous. Midazolam, for example, can be given to dental phobics who, following surgery, can remember little about what happened.[17]

A number of studies have examined the influence of benzodiazepines in relation to the distinction between implicit and explicit memory. Generally the position is that benzodiazepines affect explict memory measures (e.g. free recall) but have no influence on implicit memory measures.[18]

PSYCHOGENIC LOSS OF MEMORY

All the above examples of memory loss involve some interference, either temporary or permanent, with the biological working of the brain. For this reason these types of memory disorder are called **organic**. However, there are other classes of memory disorder known as **functional** or **psychogenic** in which the cause is not attributed to any obvious brain malfunction. It must be stated from the outset that these disorders are rare and anyone purporting to show them should be treated with a healthy degree of scepticism. The reason for this is that media portrayals of memory loss typically choose the psychogenic form because of its dramatic potential. A good example is Wim Wenders' film *Paris, Texas* in which the central figure gradually regains memory of the past. It is not surprising, therefore, that people deciding to simulate a memory disorder base it on media depictions rather than medical cases.

Despite these reservations there do appear to be genuine cases of psychogenic memory loss and all of them are distinguished by preceding negative life events such as exposure to violence and bereavement. The commonest form is **dissociative** or **hysterical amnesia** in which a section or more of a person's past is suppressed. This is commonly observed in survivors of armed combat and people who have committed murder. Ian Brady is a good example in that he suppressed the memory of his horrific murder of children before remembering many years later where he had buried their bodies. The more recent and highly publicised case of Mary Bell also reveals how she suppressed her memory for killing two little boys when she was 11 years old:

> The most important development in Mary's mind during the months of remand and the weeks of the trial was that she began to dissociate herself from her own acts. In the beginning she did this deliberately, and consciously, with quite remarkable dexterity, as Chief Inspector Dobson would describe, noting her clever lies. Eventually, however, the psychological blocking mechanism which protects the mind from the unbearable took over and made this dissociation real.[19]

Much rarer is the phenomenon of **fugue** in which a person forgets his or her personal identity. Very little is known about this condition because there have been few opportunities for controlled investigation. **Multiple personality (MP)** is the third form of psychogenic disorder and it is truly strange. A person with MP has a number of different personalities who have varying access to one another—one personality will know about the existence of the others but not vice versa.[20] MP seems to be a way of enabling a disturbed individual to compartmentalise different aspects of a troubled past. However, there are many who do not believe that MP is genuine and they cite the fact that the number of people presenting with MP has grown enormously in the last few years, as has the number of personalities possessed by a given individual. Instead, it is argued that multiple personality is one example of a mass cultural hysteria which also embraces phenomena such "recovered" memory of sexual abuse— see Chapter 7—and the growing number of people claiming to have been abducted by aliens.[21]

Repression

Some of you will have noticed that I have used the word "suppression" to account for inhibited memories. Some authors might be tempted to use the term "repression". I have avoided this because it is linked directly to Freud's concept of forgetting, which was intimately bound up with his theory of psycho-sexual development. Briefly, Freud believed that people went through four stages of development, oral, anal, oedipal and sexual. During the oral stage attention was focused on the nipple and sucking and then in the anal phase toilet training became dominant. The oedipal stage represented the dawning of sexual feeling and, in males, led to sexual focusing on mother with accompanying guilt about how the father would feel. This oedipal conflict was resolved by the castration complex in which desire for the mother is overcome by fear of castration. With the oedipal conflict resolved the person passes to the sexual stage. Freud argued that if the oedipal conflict was not resolved then repression of those events would occur and regression to either the anal or oral phase would take place—not literally but in terms of symbolic behaviour like excessive tidiness or drinking too much.

Freud's idea of repression does not carry a lot of weight. It was never demonstrated exactly how the theory worked for females—experiments to show that oedipal conflict information can be repressed failed, and it is very difficult to see how the repression mechanism could be a general account of forgetting.

However, this leaves begging what the concept of "suppression" is. My recent study of a woman may give some clues. We will see in the next chapter that the frontal lobes are the strategic centre for memory; they guide what goes into memory and are also crucially involved in the retrieval process. The woman I studied, Elizabeth, had a traumatic life history involving attempts on her life and the death of a child. She was admitted to hospital unable to remember much about her past. An interesting feature of her case was that she showed marked evidence of frontal lobe dysfunction and, when this cleared, her memories returned. It is therefore conceivable that the retrieval processes in the frontal lobes might become distorted or impaired, rendering them unable to reconstruct certain types of memory.[22]

Memory in Post-traumatic Stress Disorder

Post-traumatic stress disorder (**PTSD**) is now a recognised condition that presents in an individual following a traumatic event. It is most commonly observed in combat veterans but can also be found in people who have been involved in tragic accidents involving loss of life, victims or witnesses of violent or horrific events (e.g. mass deaths at a football stadium—as occurred at Hillsborough), or been subjected to sexual abuse as a child. The effects of PTSD on memory are somewhat complex. Typically the sufferer is amnesic for the traumatic experiences but, from time to time, **flashbacks** occur in which the traumatic experience is vividly recreated in the individual's mind. What determines a flashback is not clear but one factor appears to be mood.

Memory is known to be sensitive to **state dependency** in that a memory is more likely to be retrieved if the individual's mood state matches that experienced at the time of the traumatic experience. There is also some suggestion that recall of traumatic memories have a "dissociative quality" in that the person attributes the traumatic recall to a personal aspect that is in some way detached from their normal ongoing self.

There is now abundant evidence that PTSD victims also have impaired ability to remember new information. For example, Vietnam veterans with PTSD performed more poorly than controls on components of the Wechsler Memory Scale, and this type of effect has been shown on a variety of other tests of memory. Adolescent victims of violence in Beirut with PTSD have been shown to achieve lower academic performance than their counterparts without PTSD. Victims of PTSD also exhibit "memory gaps" ranging from minutes to hours in which they wander aimlessly and "come to" often many miles away with no idea how they got there. Also, consistent with the state-dependency view of PTSD, victims of PTSD show **greater** recall of trauma-related words but poorer recall of neutral and positive affect words.

There is now a great deal of knowledge about why stress causes loss of memory function[23]. Stress is known to increase the levels of neurochemicals known as **glucocorticoids** and that this in turn has adverse effects on memory. There is a disorder known as the Morbus–Cushing syndrome which results in abnormally high levels of **cortisol** production, and patients with this disorder exhibit memory dysfunction as one of their primary symptoms. Cortisol is widely held to exert its adverse effects on a brain region known as the **hippocampus**. This structure, located bilaterally in the medial temporal lobes, is critically involved in the initial consolidation of memory and is also thought to mediate storage of memories for some time after their initial registration. Animal studies have shown that increased cortisol levels result in loss of hippocampal neurones and a decrease in dendritic branching. This loss is thought to be attributable to an increased vulnerability of the hippocampus to endogenously generated amino acids. Further evidence for the effects of cortisol on the hippocampus comes from studies showing that it has a major effect of the neurochemistry of hippocampal function.

Other research also points towards a critical relationship between stress and hippocampal function. Monkeys exposed to stress as a result of overcrowding were found to have hippocampal damage and there is similar evidence in humans. One study used magnetic resonance imaging (MRI) to compare hippocampal volume in Vietnam veterans with PTSD and healthy subjects. The PTSD veterans were found to have an 8% reduction in the volume of the right hippocampus with no changes in adjacent brain structures. Similarly, using positron emission tomography (PET), Vietnam veterans with PTSD were found to have reduced blood flow in the hippocampus, again indicating a degree of malfunction. The same research group has found a selective 17% reduction in the left hippocampus of adult survivors of sexual abuse.

The above studies point to permanent changes in brain structure caused by stress and presumably mediated, at least in part, by prolonged exposure to elevated cortisol levels. However, there is also evidence that increased cortisol levels can also cause temporary memory impairment. Public speaking, for example, can induce varying degrees of stress in people and it has been found that, immmediately following speaking, those with higher stress indicated by raised cortisol levels, had poorer memory.

SUMMARY

- The causes of memory loss are many and varied but can be divided into permanent and transient disorders.
- Head injury takes two forms, penetrating and closed. The effects of the latter are often far more devastating.
- There are many forms of encephalitis that can cause memory loss. The most severe of these is herpes simplex encephalitis.

- Alcohol consumption, per se, can disrupt memory but severe memory loss only arises if it gives rise to Korsakoff's syndrome.
- Strokes and aneurysms are another major cause of memory impairment.
- There are many illnesses that produce dementia and accompanying memory loss. The most common of these is Alzheimer's disease.
- ECT causes a temporary disruption of memory but there is no reliable evidence that it harms memory permanently.
- TGA and TEA are both conditions that cause a temporary disruption of memory.
- Memory loss of non-organic origin is known as functional or organic amnesia. There are several forms: dissociative amnesia, fugue and multiple personality. Diagnosis is difficult.
- Repression, as defined by Freud, lacks scientific support but some concept of suppression is needed to explain genuine psychogenic amnesia.

NOTES AND REFERENCES

1. Some people would question this statement and claim that retrograde amnesia can exist in the absence of any retrograde impairment. My own opinion is that this view is erroneous and that when cases of this type present they are either the result of malingering or psychogenic memory loss (see later in the chapter). Parkin, A.J. (1996) Focal retrograde amnesia: A multi-faceted deficit? *Acta Neuropathologica Belgica*, **96**, 43–50.
2. Parkin, A.J. & Hunkin, N.M. (1991) Memory loss following radiation therapy for naso-pharyngeal cancer. *British Journal of Clinical Psychology*, **30**, 349–357. A comprehensive guide to memory disorders, common and uncommon, is provided by Kapur, N. (1988) *Memory Disorders in Clinical Practice*, Hove: Erlbaum.

3. Squire, L.R. et al. (1989) Description of brain injury in the amnesic patient NA based on magnetic resonance imaging. *Experimental Neurology*, **105**, 23–35. Dusoir, H. et al. (1990) The role of diencephalic pathology in human memory disorder. *Brain*, **113**, 1695–1706. See also Kapur op. cit.[2] for an overview of penetrating head injury.

4. The most recent comprehensive review of closed head injury and memory is provided by Richardson, J.T.E. (1990) *Clinical and Neuropsychological Aspects of Closed Head Injury*. London: Taylor & Francis.

5. An extensive account of memory loss following herpes simplex encephalitis is provided by Parkin, A.J. & Leng, N.R.C. (1993) *Neuropsychology of the Amnesic Syndrome*, chap 6. Hove: Erlbaum. See also Utley, T. et al. (1997) The long-term neuropsychological outcome of herpes simplex encephalitis in a series of unselected survivors. *Neuropsychiatry, Neuropsychology, and Behavioural Neurology*, **10**, 180–189.

6. A comprehensive account of alcohol and memory can be found in Knight, R.G. & Longmore, B.E. (1994) *Clinical Neuropsychology of Alcoholism*. Hove: Erlbaum.

7. There are a number of accounts of Korsakoff's Syndrome. Kapur, op. cit.[2] Knight & Longmore op. cit.[6] and Parkin & Leng, op. cit.[5] all have accounts of the disorder. See also Kopelman, M.D. (1995) Korsakoff's Syndrome. *British Journal of Psychiatry*, **166**, 154–173.

8. See Kapur op. cit.[2] and Parkin & Leng op. cit.[5] for a more extensive account of these disorders. See also Diamond, B.J. et al. (1997) Memory and executive functions in amnesic and non amnesic patients with aneurysms of the anterior communicating artery. *Brain*, **120**, 1015–1025.

9. A good overview of memory disorder in most kinds of dementia can be found in Brandt, J. & Rich, J.B. (1995) Memory disorders in the dementias. In A.D. Baddeley et al. (eds) *Handbook of Memory Disorders*. Chichester: Wiley. See also Cherry, K.E. & Plauche, M.F. (1996) Memory impairment in Alzheimer's Disease. Findings, interventions, and implications. *Journal of Clinical Geropsychology*, **2**, 263–296. Parks, R.W. et al. (eds) (1993) *Neuropsychology of Alzheimer's*

Disease and other Dementias. New York: Oxford University Press.

10. A recent account of ECT and memory is provided in my book Parkin, A.J. (1997) *Memory & Amnesia: An Introduction,* chap. 9. Oxford: Basil Blackwell.

11. For a recent update on this puzzling disorder, see Hodges, J.R. (1998) Unravelling the enigma of transient global amnesia. *Annals of Neurology,* **43,** 151–153.

12. Kapur, N. (1993) Transient epileptic amnesia: A clinical update and reformulation. *Journal of Neurology, Neurosurgery and Psychiatry,* **56,** 1184–1190. Zeman et al. (1998) Transient epileptic amnesia: A description of the clinical and neuropsychological features in 10 cases and a review of the literature. *Journal of Neurology, Neurosurgery and Psychiatry,* **68,** 435–443. More generally epilepsy has deleterious effects on memory. Little is recalled of events during a fit (the ictal phase) and memory can also remain disturbed during the fit free (inter-ictal) phase with deficits being particularly likely in patients whose epilepsy stems solely from temporal lobe disruption. For a review of the effects of epilepsy, per se, on memory ability see Kapur, op. cit.[2]

13. Abel, E.L. (1971) Marijuana and memory. Acquisition or retrieval? *Science,* **173,** 1038–1040.

14. Darley, C.F. et al. (1974) Influence of marijuana on storage and retrieval processes in memory. *Memory and Cognition,* **1,** 196–200. More recent studies of marijuana indicate that the deficits induced by heavy marijuana use (smoking every day) extend beyond impairments of memory to affect a wide range of mental abilities: Pope, H.G. & Yurgelun-Todd, D. (1996) The residual cognitive effects of heavy marijuana use. *Journal of the American Medical Association,* **27,** 521–527. It has also been suggested that marijuana causes changes in brain function which outlast the direct effects of the drug: Block, R.I. (1996) Does heavy marijuana use impair human cognition and brain function? *Journal of the American Medical Association,* **27,** 560–561.

15. File, S.E. & Bond, A.J. (1979) Impaired performance and sedation after a single dose of lorazepam. *Psychopharmacology,* **66,** 309–313.

16. Brown, J. et al. (1983) Effects of lorazepam on rate of forget-ting, on semantic memory and on manual dexterity. *Neuropsychologia*, **21**, 501–512.
17. Bigl, P. et al. (1992) Our experience of midazolam and flumazenil in dentistry. *Current Therapeutic Research*, **51**, 92–96.
18. Polster, M.R. (1993) Drug-induced amnesia: implications for cognitive neuropsychological investigations. *Psychological Bulletin*, **114**, 477–493.
19. Sereny, G. (1998) *Cries Unheard*. London: Macmillan.
20. For reviews of psychogenic amnesia, see Kihlstrom, J.F. & Schacter, D.L. (1995) Functional disorders of auto-biographical memory. In A.D. Baddeley et al. (eds) *Handbook of Memory Disorders*. Chichester: Wiley. While there seems a general tendency to accept the validity of psycho-genic amnesic states, (e.g. Arrigo, J.-M. & Pezdek, K. (1998) Lessons from the study of psychogenic amnesia. *Current Directions in Psychological Science*, **6**, 148–152), there are oth-ers who claim that there is no such thing and that apparent psychogenic states arise because people choose not to re-port painful memories rather than suppress them (Pope, H.G. et al. (1998) Questionable validity of "dissociative am-nesia" in trauma victims. *British Journal of Psychiatry*, **172**, 210–215).
21. This point is made particularly strongly by Showalter, E. (1997) *Hystories: Hysterical Epidemics and Modern Culture*. New York: Columbia University Press.
22. Parkin, A.J. & Stampfer, H. (1995) Keeping out the past. In R. Campbell & M. Conway (eds) *Broken Memories*. Oxford: Basil Blackwell.
23. There are many references to the effects of stress on mem-ory. A useful introduction is Parkin, A.J. (2000) Stress and memory impairment. In F. Finke (ed.) *Encyclopedia of Stress*. San Diego, CA: Academic Press. Other more detailed refer-ences are: Bremner, J.D. & Narayan, M. (1998) The effects of stress on memory and the hippocampus throughout the life cycle: Implications for childhood development and aging. *Development and Psychopathology*, **10**, 871–885. Bremner, J.D.

et al. (1995) Functional neuroanatomical correlates of the effects of stress on memory. *Journal of Traumatic Stress*, **8**, 527–553. Lupien, S.J. et al. (1997) Stress-induced declarative memory impairment in healthy elderly subjects: Relationship to cortisol reactivity. *Journal of Clinical Neuroendrocrinology and Metabolism*, **82**, 2070–2075. Van der Kolk, B.A. et al. (eds) (1996) *Traumatic Stress: The Effects of Overwhelming Experience on Mind, Body and Society*. New York: Guilford Press.

6

UNDERSTANDING AND COPING WITH MEMORY LOSS

The previous chapter introduced us to the wide range of different causes of memory loss. In this chapter I want to go into more detail about the psychological characteristics of memory loss and end with a discussion of what can be done to help a person who is suffering significant memory failure.

WHAT FORMS OF MEMORY ARE AFFECTED?

In Chapter 1 we saw that memory is divided into short-term and long-term store (STS and LTS) and that the latter itself divides into procedural, semantic and episodic memory—although some theorists prefer to lump the latter two together as declarative memory. There is plenty of evidence that the various agents that cause memory loss do not affect STS. Rather than review evidence from a wide range of studies I will concentrate my account on the findings from one amnesic patient who has been investigated extensively over the last 30 years[1] but I will also consider other evidence where appropriate.

HM is a man who underwent temporal lobectomy in order to cure a particularly severe form of epilepsy. The operation was successful in treating his epilepsy but had a shattering side effect in that it left him severely amnesic. As a result, HM's memory has become "frozen" in time: he has learned little about the world since the mid-1950s. He has no recollection of events such as the Vietnam War and Watergate and words such as "fax" and "CD" are meaningless.

HM has been given various tasks that are thought to tap selectively into STS. He has been given the digit-span test a number of times and on all occasions his performance has been within the normal range but his performance deteriorates markedly if the number of items he is asked to remember exceeds his measured capacity by even one digit. Normal digit span is also a characteristic of virtually all patients with significant memory loss such as those surviving encephalitis, and patients with Korsakoff's syndrome.[2] The only exception to this rule is patients with dementia where a downturn in digit span can be expected as the disease progresses. On the probe-digit procedure HM showed normal performance with four or less intervening digits, but a drastic drop in performance with higher numbers of digits. This again indicates normal performance on the part of the task thought to reflect STS but impairments when LTS.[3]

The recency effect in free recall (see Chapter 1) is also considered to reflect short-term storage processes. HM has never done this task but plenty of other amnesic subjects have. Figure 6.1 shows the results from an experiment that compared a group of amnesic patients who had lost their memory from various causes with a group of control subjects. The results are very clear: amnesics show a normal recency effect but impairment in

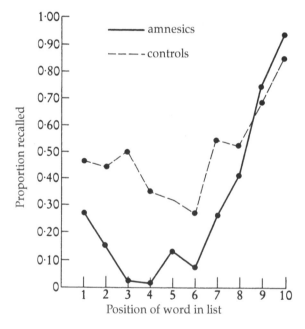

Figure 6.1: Results of an experiment comparing amnesic and normal people on free recall. Note that the amnesics and controls do not differ in terms of a recency effect but that anmesics recall far less from earlier parts of the list.

earlier parts of the curve thought to involve LTS, thus indicating preserved STS function.

In sum there is little disagreement that most of the agents that cause memory impairment do not affect STS function and that the deficit lies in the function of LTS.

THE NATURE OF LTS IMPAIRMENT IN AMNESIA

HM's inability to commit new information to memory, ante-rograde amnesia, is startling. Suzanne Corkin, who has done a great deal of work with HM, notes that he

> still . . . does not know where he lives, who cares for him, or where he ate his last meal. His guesses as to the current year may be as much as 43 years off . . . In 1982 he did not recognise a picture of himself that had been taken on his 40th birthday in 1966.[4]

More formally HM's memory for a wide variety of material has been studied, and regardless of the type of material (e.g. abstract patterns, common objects, maze solutions or locations) his forgetting of this information is total within minutes. Anterograde amnesia is the hallmark of almost all memory disorders and there are numerous demonstrations in the literature of poor long-term retention of new information by amnesic sufferers. Measures of free recall are the most sensitive and it is not uncommon to find patients who can recall little or nothing of a word list presented several minutes earlier. Recognition memory is also very poor with patients, often producing performance levels no better than guessing. These experimental findings are complemented by clinical observations that these patients also have immense difficulty learning new names and finding their way around new surroundings.[5]

EPISODIC VERSUS SEMANTIC MEMORY

While there is no doubt about the severity of anterograde impairment there is some discussion as to how this impairment might
best be described. Chapter 1 introduced us to the episodic–
semantic memory distinction with the former representing personal event memory and the latter language, concepts and general knowledge about the world. At a clinical level amnesic
patients come over very much as being impaired on episodic
tasks. At an informal level they forget day-to-day events with
amazing ease and experimental demonstrations of their forgetful-
ness emphasise tasks involving episodic memory (e.g. did I show
you this picture 5 minutes ago? etc.). In contrast, general language
and intellectual skills can often seem unimpaired.

Semantic memory, at least on the surface, seems to be relatively
unimpaired thus providing a potential argument that amnesia is
essentially a deficit in episodic memory. Considering HM first, he
has a recorded WAIS IQ (see Chapter 4) of 122. If one considers a
wide-ranging intelligence test as a good measure of semantic
memory because it tests vocabulary, general knowledge, arithme-
tic and problem-solving skills, etc., then HM would appear to
have preserved semantic memory. Normal or near-normal levels
of IQ have also been recorded for many other patients, suggesting
again that semantic memory is unimpaired.[6]

There are, however, difficulties in ascribing all amnesics'
memory difficulties to a problem with episodic memory. If correct, one would expect amnesic patients to acquire new semantic
memory but, generally speaking, this is not the case. Above we
saw that HM's experience has not allowed him to learn new
vocabulary and concentrated efforts within the laboratory have
also failed in their attempts to teach him new words. Similar
failures have been reported in other studies.[7] However, one
can argue that this is not particularly good evidence. Perhaps
episodic memory is needed in the initial stages of vocabulary
acquisition. For many of you, for example, "hippocampus" is a
new word and in order to retrieve its meaning you may, in the
initial stages, need to remember your specific encounter with it

in this book until its memory sinks properly into semantic memory. However, when we look at another dimension of the amnesic deficit the episodic–semantic distinction becomes much more difficult to accept.

RETROGRADE AMNESIA

When brain damage results in the loss of memories acquired before an injury, this is known as **retrograde amnesia**. In Chapter 4 we noted the Autobiographical Memory Interview as one way of measuring retrograde deficits and there are a number of alternative ways. One way is to ask people to identify pictures of famous people from the past or, alternatively, to show them pictures of famous events and ask them to describe what is happening. These tests are always designed so that information from different time periods is sampled (see Figure 6.2) . This enables the measurement of any temporal gradient that might be present. As we saw in Chapter 4 it is generally the case that older memories are less vulnerable to brain damage than those formed nearer the time that illness or injury affected memory— something that is termed a **temporal gradient** (see Figure 6.2).

Studies of retrograde amnesia indicate that it is extremely variable, depending on the cause of memory loss. In the case of HM there is some dispute. Initial measures suggested that his retrograde deficit went back only two years prior to his operation, but later studies have suggested that it is more extensive. Relatively recently HM attended his high school reunion but did not recognise anybody in the room. Closed head injury can produce an extremely variable pattern of retrograde impairment— the general rule being the more severe the anterograde amnesia the worse the retrograde amnesia. Other disorders, such as Korsakoff's syndrome and encephalitis, are frequently associated with marked temporal gradients and there is very little good evidence that extensive retrograde impairments can be observed without a gradient being present.[8] We still have no idea why

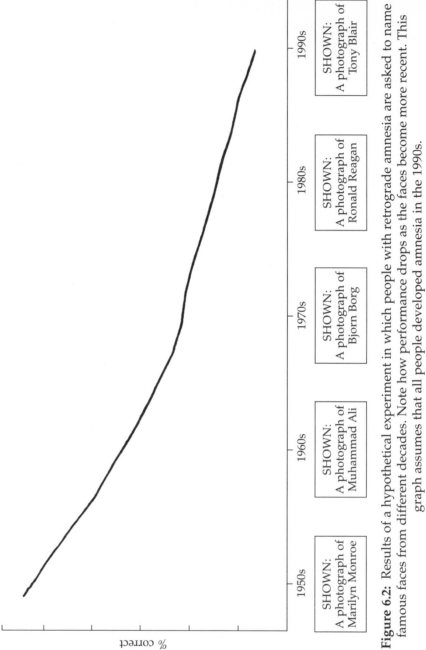

Figure 6.2: Results of a hypothetical experiment in which people with retrograde amnesia are asked to name famous faces from different decades. Note how performance drops as the faces become more recent. This graph assumes that all people developed amnesia in the 1990s.

these temporal gradients exist although one possibility is that older memories have been utilised more and have thus become more broadly represented in memory. As a result, more areas of the brain have to be damaged before the memory loss is complete. An alternative proposal is that memory consolidation is a very long process (see Chapter 1).

As indicated above the nature of retrograde amnesia has a direct bearing on our interpretation of memory deficits. If one considers some of the retrograde tests on which amnesic subjects fail, e.g. identifying faces from the past, it is not clear that this involves remembering a personal event. Consider the pictures described in Figure 6.2; would identifying them involve you in a specific personal recollection? I suspect not. Rather it represents the application of general knowledge. What then do we make of the tendency of amnesic patients to perform normally on intelligence tests? The important thing to remember is that tests like WAIS-R evaluate information and abilities that are acquired by early adulthood. As a result, the test is examining early memories, i.e. ones that would be least affected by temporal gradients. Recent studies have confirmed that there is a temporal gradient in semantic memory if one considers memories formed later in life.[9] In one famous study an amnesic professor was found to have temporally graded deficits in both episodic memory and semantic memory—the latter reflected in his inability to define terms used in his specialist subject.[10]

The above considerations lead us to conclude that amnesics show a deficit in declarative memory which, as you will recall, is any memory that can be consciously accessed. This leads us neatly to consider the converse of declarative memory—procedural memory.

PROCEDURAL MEMORY

HM has shown preserved procedural learning in a variety of situations. Informally it has been noted that he has learned how

to assemble a collapsible wheelchair. In the laboratory he has
shown normal performance on various tests of motor skills. One
of these is the pursuit rotor task in which the subject holds a
stylus emitting a light beam and has to keep the beam in contact
with an erratically moving light beam. HM learned to perform
exceptionally well on this even though each time he encountered the test he claimed never to have done it before.[11] Preser-
vations similar to HM have been noted in many other studies.
One study, for example, showed that a man rendered severely
amnesic due to encephalitis could still learn new tunes on the
piano even though his memory for turning up for band practice
was poor![12]

IMPLICIT VERSUS EXPLICIT MEMORY

This distinction was considered in Chapter 2. To recap, the
implicit–explicit distinction is an approach to the study of memory based on the demands of tasks. An implicit memory task is
one that indirectly assesses whether an event has influenced an
individual, whereas an explicit task requires the subject to recollect consciously a specific event—explicit memory is therefore part of what we have called declarative memory.

HM has shown implicit memory in a variety of studies.[13] In
one study he was shown a series of degraded pictures which
were made systematically more informative until he identified
them. The pictures were subsequently represented and it was
found that HM, despite being unable to recognise any of the
pictures, needed less informative versions of the pictures to
achieve accurate identification. There are many examples of
other amnesic patients showing preserved implicit memory.[14]
In Chapter 4 we encountered the **stem completion** task in which
words are pre-exposed, e.g. REASON followed by a "word
puzzle" in which subjects are asked to complete incomplete
words, e.g. REA___?, with the first word that comes to mind.
Completion of the stem with the pre-exposed word, known as

priming, is indicative of implicit memory and several studies have shown normal performance on this task by amnesic subjects. **Preference judgements** are another way of measuring implicit memory. Briefly, it can be shown that people will often prefer something they have been previously exposed to even though they do not remember seeing it. In one experiment Korsakoff patients heard novel melodies. In a subsequent test they preferred these novel melodies to ones they had not heard before, even though they did not recognise them.[15]

There are also demonstrations that amnesics are capable of more complex implicit memory. One study showed amnesic patients ambiguous sentences such as "The haystack was important because the cloth ripped"—a sentence that only makes sense with the accompanying word "parachute". Patients were initially exposed to the sentences and their solution words and then asked to explain the sentences again at intervals of up to one week. The amnesic patients were able to solve previously exposed sentences much more quickly and this effect was similar for severely amnesic and moderately amnesic subjects—thus indicating that explicit memory had nothing to do with it.[16] This experiment indicates that implicit memory is very durable and this is backed up strongly in a study involving an amnesic patient known as KC. He was shown pictures, e.g. a hospital setting, alongside a related sentence "Medicine cured hiccup". After one year he could still reliably produce the last word of the sentence when presented with the rest of the information.[17]

WHAT HAS GONE WRONG IN AMNESIA?

The above account has indicated the forms of memory that are preserved or lost in amnesia but it does not explain the reason. Why is the acquisition and retrieval declarative memory selectively affected? Perhaps the most straightforward explanation is that people with amnesia fail to form new permanent memory, i.e. they have a deficit in **consolidation**. There is certainly some credibility to this theory. In Chapter 1 we saw that the hippo-campus is vital for memory and animal experiments have shown that it is particularly active during the initial stages of learning—thus suggesting that it is involved in setting up new memories. However, a failure of consolidation cannot be the only factor causing memory impairments. Studies of retrograde amnesia show that the deficit often extends back over 20 years. While it is the case that consolidation may be a longer process than we have previously thought (see Chapter 1) it seems un-likely that it would still be occurring at these very long intervals. We must therefore argue for at least one additional factor affect-ing memory.

From a common-sense point of view we can also argue for amnesia arising from a **storage deficit**—i.e. damage to the struc-tures in the cortex which hold permanent memory. Support for this comes from the fact that severe retrograde amnesia is most often, although not always, associated with extensive cortical damage. Storage deficit accounts are, in some ways a default option in that it is impossible to prove that a memory no longer exists. Concerns of this kind have led to the **retrieval deficit** account of amnesia, which argues that amnesics have defective retrieval mechanisms. This theory does not, however, get very far because, if correct, it would predict that the extent of ante-rograde and retrograde amnesia would be similar since, pre-sumably, both rely on the same retrieval mechanism. However, this does not occur and severe anterograde amnesia can often be observed in the presence of a mild retrograde amnesia and, to some extent, vice versa.

Currently the most accepted approach to explaining amnesia is that it represents a failure to encode the context of events. This theory has, however, only been developed as an account of ante-rograde amnesia and, when applied to retrograde amnesia it has been found invalid. Briefly the theory proposes that people with amnesia fail to encode information associated with an event, such as its time and place of occurrence, which in turn prevents them from forming good memories. There is some evidence for this. Amnesics have, for example, been shown to have good memories when asked whether or not they have seen something before but then fail miserably when asked either where or when that thing was presented. The context theory does, therefore, have some credibility but is limited in that it can only explain amnesia arising from damage to the diencephalon (e.g. Korsakoff's syndrome). A different explanation is needed for people with temporal lobe lesions (e.g. encephalitis) and here a consolidation defect looks more plausible.[18]

MEMORY LOSS FOLLOWING FRONTAL LOBE DAMAGE

Until relatively recently the frontal lobes of the brain were not considered important for memory. The frontal lobes were seen as the seat of the highest mental abilities such as thinking and reasoning. However, it is now known that damage to the frontal lobes can have striking effects on memory which are rather different to those found following, for example, encephalitis and Korsakoff's syndrome.[19] In particular, the frontal lobes are associated with a phenomenon known as **confabulation**. This was once described as "honest lying" and involves the production of memories which are clearly false but which the patient believes to be true.[20] Very often they are an attempt to blend existing circumstances with more remote memories, resulting in a bizarre output. One patient I studied was in a mental hospital but attempted to impose memories of his school days as an attempt to explain his current existence. Here is part of his account:

AP: *Tell me a bit about (name of hospital).*

JB: *Well it's a nuthouse for want of a better phrase—lunatic asylum I would imagine.*

AP: *What makes you say that?*

JB: *There's some funny people in there. I want out.*

AP: *You were telling me about (name of hospital). Why do you think you're there?*

JB: *I don't really know. I have asked several people but never got an answer that satisfies me. Don't know why I'm there at all.*

AP: *What do you do during the day there?*

JB: *Same as everyone else. Bit of maths, bit of English, bit of religion first thing in the morning . . . depends what's on the timetable—normal school lessons.*

AP: *If it's a nuthouse why are you having lessons?*

JB: *Brain stimulation I suppose.*

AP: *Brain stimulation?*

JB: *Got to get the brain working again.*

JB's variable insight interacting with confabulation also cropped up a little later in the same conversation.

JB: *I've been chugging along over the last three weeks. . . . It's this bloody memory.*

AP: *Memory's the problem?*

JB: *Yea*

AP: *You're confused about where you are. You would like some help?*

JB: *Yea, clear the old brain from where its got clogged up.*

AP: *How often do you find yourself confused?*

JB: *Quite regularly. Sort of get in the car and think where am I going? I must sit and work it all out. But it's not as bad as all that—I'll retract that straight away.*

AP: *What helps then?*

JB: *Well I give myself a clue and I can work it out from there. Well I've got in the car and looked at my timetable where it says on the first page which school I'm going to. I haven't turned up at the wrong one yet.*

AP: *How many different schools do you go to?*

JB: *Well there's been three in as many months.*[21]

Confabulation is not well understood but what seems clear is that the confabulator is failing to monitor the appropriateness of what he or she is remembering. Tasks involving memory monitoring are typically referred to as an additional form of

metamemory. A good example of this is the **feeling of knowing** phenomenon. Imagine being asked a question such as "What does the L. stand for in L. Ron Hubbard?" You may not be able to answer it but nonetheless be able to predict how easily you would recognise the correct answer from a set of alternatives (e.g. Lancelot, *Lafayette*, Lionel). Studies of people with frontal lobe damage show that they are very poor at predicting their own memory performance because they seem unable to monitor the contents of their own memory.[22] A related phenomenon is **source monitoring** in which people have to decide which of two sources was the origin of something they know. Again it has been shown that frontal damage impedes the ability to remember the source of information even though the information itself may be well remembered. Linked to this, frontal lobe damage also seems to have a dramatic effect on people's ability to remember the **temporal order** (i.e. time-based) of events.[23]

There has been quite a lot of work recently comparing recall and recognition in frontal patients and a number of reports that these individuals show normal recognition but poor recall. This contrasts with the more usual situation in which a memory-impaired person has deficits in both forms of memory.[24] However, this view of normal recognition memory needs to be treated carefully because it has been shown that, although these people identify things they have been shown at normal levels, they tend to wrongly identify things they have not been shown. The poor recall, however, seems undeniable and it seems due to some impairment in retrieval strategy—for some reason the retrieval mechanism cannot get going. It is thus characteristic of frontal patients that they often show much better recall when given a prompt.[25]

WHAT GOES WRONG IN FRONTAL LOBE MEMORY DISORDER?

The commonest approach to thinking about why frontal lobe damage affects memory the way it does revolves around the idea that the frontal lobes act as an **executive**. As we saw above, the frontal lobe is known to be involved in thinking, planning, and decision making and it is not difficult to see how the elements involved in these complex tasks might also be relevant to memory function.[26] At various points in this book we have emphasised that retrieval is a reconstructive process where, in effect, the memory system has to establish a hypothesis about what it is looking for and then confirm that the retrieved information is correct (verification). It is not difficult to see how components of thinking, planning and decision making might be involved in this retrieval process. For example, impairments in planning might lead to inappropriate or impoverished retrieval strategies.

This idea can also be extended to cover encoding—the processes that determine how an item is stored in memory. In order to find a memory subsequently it is essential that it is stored away in a distinct place that easily enables it to be distinguished from other memories of a similar type. Presumably this function must also rely on frontal lobe function because appropriate storage must be reliant on higher order processes. The involvement of the frontal lobes in both retrieval and encoding has recently been confirmed by studies of **functional neuroimaging** in which the activity of a person's brain is measured while he or she is carrying out a particular task. Using this method it has been shown that the left side of the frontal lobes is particularly active during learning, whereas the right is dominant when retrieval is occurring.[27]

We know, therefore, that damage to the frontal lobes can disrupt both encoding and retrieval processes but a further question is: Why has this occurred? One influential idea is that the memory problems experienced by frontal patients, and indeed many of their other problems, stem from a fundamental problem in focusing **attention**. In order to be efficient in any mental task we need to focus on the essential elements of a task—solving a written problem, for example, is not facilitated if we allocate to deciding the shade of azure that the problem is written on. The same applies to memory. If we give as much weight to irrelevant detail as we do to key aspects of what we are trying to remember, then our memory will be poor. There is now plenty of evidence that frontal lobe damage results in enhanced distractibility and that the poor attentional focusing indicated by this lies at the heart of memory problems experienced by people with frontal lobe damage.[27]

HELPING SOMEONE WITH MEMORY LOSS

Memory loss arises through the irreversible damage to brain tissue. For this reason it was thought for a long time that nothing could really be done to help someone who had suffered memory impairment. However, our greater understanding of memory has revised this position and there is now scope for providing at least some help to those afflicted with loss of memory.[29]

The first approach combines common sense with the variety of external aids that are available to help people with poor memories. There is much around the environment that can be altered to help a memory-impaired person. Labelling can be employed on cupboards and signs can be used as reminders in significant places (e.g. a sign saying "don't forget your key" at the door). The use of written diaries or other reminders about forthcoming events can be very useful and a notepad by the phone is useful for message taking. Routine is very important because there is plenty of evidence that even people with severe memory loss can get used to a routine. In line with this it is also important to keep the location of things in the environment constant. Poster boards with the names and photographs of family and friends can be helpful for those with retrograde amnesia.[30]

External aids can be as simple as a diary but some research has shown that amnesic people can make use of electronic personal organisers. However, due to the additional deficits that some patients suffer, they are not all able to learn how to use these pieces of equipment. Perhaps the most difficult of these additional deficits is that many memory-impaired people lack any **insight** into their problems. Believing they do not have a problem thus makes it especially difficult to get them to learn to use strategies.[31]

Time-based reminding devices are useful and there has recently been a great deal of success with one known as "Neuropage". This operates like a paging device and, following a signal, displays instructions to an amnesic person at different times of the day. Studies have shown that this acts as a very useful cueing device and can impart a considerable degree of independence to a memory-impaired person.[32]

When research into memory remediation began in the 1980s there was a great deal of interest in **memory strategies** or **mnemonic aids** as a way of helping to improve memory.[33] It is often thought that memory is rather like a muscle—the more you use it the stronger it gets. Unfortunately this is not the case and memory will only improve through repetition if that leads to more efficient strategies evolving. Sometimes strategies can evolve on their own—e.g. someone may start to make links between the things they are remembering but mainly the **mnemonic** (memory aid) is provided. The most commonly explored mnemonic with the memory impaired is **mental imagery**. The use of imagery goes back to the ancient Greeks and involves the construction of mental pictures as a means of remembering. One particular technique is the **method of loci** in which a series of to-be-remembered items (e.g. a shopping list) are imagined in a particular location (e.g. different positions in the living room). Experiments showed that amnesic people could improve their memories using this method as well as other mnemonic aids involving imagery. A problem, however, is that amnesics fail to use these methods spontaneously—often due to insight problems—thus severely limiting their value. A further difficulty with using images is that they may not be precise enough. One man, for example, was taught to remember the name of his social worker, Mary Thorne, by associating her face with an image of a thorn with a smiling face. This led him to believe that the name of his social worker was "Gay Holly".

An alternative approach to memory remediation has been to devise learning strategies for amnesics that apparently rely on their preserved implicit memory. A lot of work made use of the "vanishing cues" technique which bears some resemblance to the stem completion procedure (see above).[34] The studies were practical in their orientation and involved the learning of computer vocabulary. The technique basically involved showing the person a statement such as "The command for storing information is SAVE" and then repeating the question with one letter less, e.g. SAV. If the person is correct the question is repeated until the term can be produced without any letters being present. Initial studies showed that this was more effective than standard remote learning methods and it was even used to train a densely amnesic woman as a computer operator. However, the technique is quite complicated to implement and more recent studies have not shown it to be any more effective than rote learning.

The most recent development in memory remediation has been the method of **errorless learning**.[35] This acknowledges the point that if a memory-impaired person makes a mistake, e.g. calling "Mary" "Margaret", that error will uncannily stick in memory and interfere with new learning. Several studies have now shown that this technique confers considerable advantage over learning methods that allow the generation of errors. In the laboratory setting the method has been shown to be a more effective means of learning pairs of words and unfamiliar face name pairs. Errorless learning has also been used in more applied settings. We have used it successfully to reteach a man the names of politicians he had forgotten, and we have also shown that the method can be used to teach word-processing skills. Here we should acknowledge that the vanishing cues technique has also been successful in this respect. We have also looked into the issue of whether errorless learning is making use of preserved implicit memory. Unfortunately our studies have shown that the technique tends to exploit the amount of residual explicit memory the person has available.[36]

SUMMARY

- Amnesia is an impairment in LTS function.
- The LTS impairment is most apparent for episodic kinds of information.

- Retrograde amnesia shows a temporal gradient with older memories being less vulnerable to brain insult.
- Retrograde amnesia affects both episodic and semantic memory thus undermining the distinction and instead suggesting a single, declarative, memory system.
- Procedural memory and implicit memory are largely unaffected in amnesia.
- Amnesia may have a variety of causes, including consolidation and storage. Investigations of the latter suggest that amnesics may have a specific problem in storing the context associated with information they try to learn.
- Damage to the frontal lobes causes a different kind of memory disorder associated with confabulation, and difficulties with metamemory, source memory and memory for temporal order.
- Frontal lobe memory disorders are often attributed to failure of the executive system governing all higher mental abilities. One aspect of this executive function may involve the appropriate allocation of attentional resources.
- Common-sense strategies can do a lot to help the memory-impaired person.
- A variety of external aids are available to help those with memory problems.
- Various learning strategies can help with memory problems but amnesics rarely use them spontaneously.
- Vanishing cues and errorless learning techniques represent new ways of helping amnesics to retain new information.

NOTES AND REFERENCES

1. By any standards HM is an extraordinary patient and there are numerous accounts in the literature. The most thorough are: Corkin, S. (1984) Lasting consequences of medial temporal lobectomy: Clinical course and experimental findings in case HM. *Seminars in Neurology*, **4**, 249–259. Ogden, J. &

Corkin, S. (1991) Memories of HM. In W.C. Abrahams et al. (eds) *Memory Mechanisms: A Tribute to G.V. Goddard*. Hillsdale, NJ: Erlbaum. Parkin, A.J. (1996) HM: The medial temporal lobes and memory. In C. Code et al. (eds) *Classic Cases in Neuropsychology*. Hove: Psychology Press.

2. See Parkin, A.J. & Leng, N.R.C. (1993) *Neuropsychology of the Amnesic Syndrome*. Hove: Erlbaum. This book provides systematic coverage of STS and LTS function in various forms of amnesia.

3. Wicklegren, W.A. (1968) Sparing of short-term memory in an amnesic patient. *Neuropsychologia*, **6**, 235–244.

4. Corkin (1984) op. cit.[1]

5. My own book with Leng (1993) op. cit.,[2] still provides the most comprehensive account of anterograde deficits in amnesia. See also Kapur, N. (1998) *Memory Disorders in Clinical Practice*. Hove: Psychology Press.

6. Parkin & Leng (1993) op. cit.[2]

7. Gabrieli, J.D.E., Cohen, N.J. & Corkin, S. (1988) The impaired learning of semantic knowledge following bilateral medial temporal lobe resection. *Brain and Cognition*, **7**, 153–177. Grossman, M. (1987) Lexical acquisition in Korsakoff's Psychosis. *Cortex*, **23**, 631–644.

8. Parkin & Leng (1993) op. cit.[2]

9. Verafeaillie, M. & Roth, H.L. (1996) Knowledge of English vocabulary in amnesia. *Journal of the International Neuropsychological Society*, **1**, 443–453.

10. Butters, N. (1984) Alcoholic Korsakoff Syndrome: An update. *Seminars in Neurology*, **4**, 226–244.

11. Parkin (1996) op. cit.[1]

12. Parkin & Leng (1993) op cit. provide extensive evidence of preserved procedural learning in amnesia.

13. Parkin (1996) op. cit.[1]

14. The first actual demonstration of this was Graf, P., Squire, L.R. & Mandler, G. (1984) The information amnesic patients do not forget. *Journal of Experimental Psychology: Learning, Memory and Cognition*, **9**, 164–178. However, a similar type of finding was reported much earlier: Warrington, E.K. & Weiskrantz, L. (1970) Amnesic syndrome: Consolidation or retrieval? *Nature*, **228**, 628–630.

15. Johnson, M.K., Kim, J.K. & Risse, G. (1985) Do alcoholic Korsakoff patients acquire affective reactions? *Journal of Experimental Psychology: Learning, Memory and Cognition*, **11**, 22–36.
16. McAndrews, M.P., Glisky, E.L. & Schacter, D.L. (1987) When priming persists: Long-lasting implicit memory for a single episode in amnesic patients. *Neuropsychologia*, **25**, 497–506.
17. Tulving, E. et al. (1991) Long lasting perceptual priming and semantic learning in amnesia. A case experiment. *Journal of Experimental Psychology: Learning, Memory and Cognition*, **17**, 595–617.
18. Recent theoretical accounts of amnesia are provided by Mayes, A.R. & Downes, J.J. (eds) (1997) *Theories of Organic Amnesia*. Hove: Psychology Press. This book is quite hard going for the novice and a simpler account can be found in Parkin, A.J. (1997) *Memory & Amnesia: An Introduction* (2nd edn), chap 6. Oxford: Blackwell.
19. For an overview of how frontal lobe damage affects memory, see Parkin (1997) op. cit.,[18] chap. 7.
20. Confabulation is a term that is often used rather broadly to mean any false information that a patient produces. More correctly it is the production of false information, usually fanciful in some way, that the patient actually believes to be true. A useful starting point for understanding confabulation is Kopelman, M.D. (1987) Two types of confabulation. *Journal of Neurology, Neurosurgery and Psychiatry*, **50**, 1482–1487. See also Schnider, A. et al. (1996) The mechanisms of spontaneous and provoked confabulations. *Brain*, **119**, 1365–1375. Benson, D.F. et al. (1996) The neural basis of confabulation. *Neurology*, **46**, 1239–1243. Confabulation is usually seen as applying to recall of personal events but it can also be observed in relation to general knowledge: Moscovitch, M. & Melo, B. (1997) Strategic retrieval and the frontal lobes. *Neuropsychologia*, **35**, 1017–1034.
21. From Parkin, A.J. (1997) The long and winding road. Twelve years of frontal amnesia. In A.J. Parkin (ed.) *Case Studies in the Neuropsychology of Memory*. Hove: Psychology Press.

22. Janowsky, J.S., Shimamura, A.P. & Squire, L.R. (1989) Memory and metamemory: Comparisons between patients with frontal lobe lesions and amnesic patients. *Psychobiology*, **7**, 3–11.
23. Janowsky, J.S., Shimamura, A.P. & Squire, L.R. (1989) Source memory impairment in patients with frontal lobe lesions. *Neuropsychologia*, **27**, 1043–1056. Milner, B. et al. (1991) Frontal lobe contribution to recency judgements. *Neuropsychologia*, **29**, 601–618.
24. Hanley, J.R. & Davies, A.D.M. (1997) Impaired recall and preserved recognition. In A.J. Parkin (ed.) *Case studies in the Neuropsychology of Memory*. Hove: Psychology Press.
25. Parkin, A.J. et al. (in press) False recognition following frontal lobe damage: The role of encoding factors. *Cognitive Neuropsychology*. Schacter, D.L. et al. (1996) False recognition and the right frontal lobe. *Neuropsychologia*, **34**, 793–808.
26. A good accessible account of the executive concept can be found in Baddeley, A.D. (1997) *Human Memory: Theory and Practice*. Hove: Psychology Press.
27. Fletcher, P.C. et al. (1995) Brain systems for encoding and retrieval of memory: An in vivo study in humans. *Brain*, **118**, 401–416. A good introduction to how these studies are done is provided by Posner, M.I. & Raichle, M.E. (1994) *Images of Mind*. New York: Freeman.
28. Shimamura, A.P. (1995) Memory and frontal lobe function. In M. Gazzaniga (ed.) *The Cognitive Neurosciences*, pp. 803–813. Cambridge, MA: MIT Press.
29. Recent reviews of memory rehabilitation include: Leon-Carrion, J. (ed.) (1997) *Neuropsychological Rehabilitation: Fundamentals, Innovations, and Directions*. Delray Beach, FL: Gr/St Lucie Press (see chap. 20). Riddoch, M.-J. and Humphreys, G.W. (eds) (1994) *Cognitive Neuropsychology and Cognitive Rehabilitation*. Hove: Erlbaum (see Part 7). Wilson, B.A. & Moffat, N. (1992) *Clinical Management of Memory Problems* (2nd edn). London: Chapman & Hall.
30. A list of common-sense advice is provided by Parkin (1997) op. cit.[18] chap. 11. A recent discussion of external memory

aids is provided by Kapur, N. (1995) Memory aids on the rehabilitation of memory disordered patients. In A.D. Baddeley et al. (eds) *Handbook of Memory Disorders*, chap. 22. Chichester: Wiley.

31. See Prigatano, G. in Leon-Carrion (1997) op. cit.[29]

32. Aldrich, F.K. (1998) Pager messages as self-reminders: A case study of their use in memory impairment. *Personal Technologies*, **2**, 1–10. Wilson, B.A. et al. (1997) Evaluation of Neuropage: A new memory aid. *Journal of Neurology, Neurosurgery and Psychiatry*, **63**, 113–115.

33. See Wilson & Moffat (1992) op cit.[29] and Parkin (1997) op. cit.[18] chap. 11.

34. See Glisky, E.L. & Schacter, D.L. (1987) Acquisition of domain specific knowledge in organic amnesia: Training for computer-related work. *Neuropsychologia*, **25**, 893–906. For an overview see Parkin (1997) op. cit.[18]

35. Baddeley, A.D. & Wilson, B.A. (1994) When implicit learning fails: Amnesia and the problem of error elimination. *Neuropsychologia*, **32**, 53–68. Squires, E.J. et al. (1997) Errorless learning of novel associations in amnesia. *Neuropsychologia*, **35**, 1103–1111.

36. Hunkin, N.M. et al. (1998) Are the benefits of errorless learning dependent on implicit memory? *Neuropsychologia*, **36,** 25–36.

7

THE FALLIBILITY OF MEMORY

When I was young, I could remember anything . . .
whether it happened or not.

(Mark Twain)

We proceed through life on the assumption that what we remember is correct. Indeed it is hard to imagine what mental life would be like if we queried the truth of everything we remembered. Yet, at the same time, we know that memory is fallible and that even convincing recollections can be wrong. The psychologist Ulric Neisser gives a good example of this. There is a memory phenomenon known as **flashbulb memory**[1] in which it is proposed that we have a particularly vivid and accurate recollection of the circumstances of hearing dramatic news such as the assassination of President Kennedy, the *Challenger* disaster, and learning about the death of Princess Diana.

Neisser's own account of a flashbulb memory goes back to his apparently clear recollection of hearing the news that the Japanese had bombed Pearl Harbor in the Second World War:

> *I recall sitting in the living room of our house . . . listening to a baseball game on the radio. The game was interrupted by an announcement of the attack, and I rushed upstairs to tell my mother. This memory has been so clear that I never questioned its inherent absurdity until last year: no one broadcasts baseball games in December!*[2]

Neisser's account introduces a golden rule about the nature of human memory: just because a memory seems vivid to a person it does not mean the memory is accurate. Take the example of John Demjanjuk who was convicted of being "Ivan the Terrible"—a man in charge of the gas chambers at Treblinka. Initially the jury was convinced by emotional eyewitness identifications who stated that you would never forget the face of someone who did so many awful things. In fact it was a misidentification based on memories that were old and unreliable.[3] It is also a mistake to consider memories associated with violence as reliable; the opposite is very much the case. A friend of mine was working in a bank when she was threatened by an unmasked man with a shotgun. After the incident she could recall nothing about his physical appearance. This type of effect has been demonstrated experimentally and shows that we must be cautious about memories formed in threatening situations.[4]

One powerful anecdote illustrating the fallibility of memory involved the Australian psychologist Don Thompson who was actively engaged in eyewitness research. As part of this research he took part in a TV discussion about eyewitnessing. A few weeks later he was picked up by the police and identified as a rapist in a line up. Fortunately for Thompson it turned out that the time of the rape incident coincided with the time he was on TV, so he had the perfect alibi. Further investigation indicated that the TV had been on during the rape and that the woman had somehow "blended" Thompson's face on TV with that of her attacker.[5]

EYEWITNESSING

Recently a survey in the USA revealed that around 77,000 people are arrested each year on the basis of eyewitness identification. However, it is also claimed that eyewitness evidence accounts for more wrongful convictions than any other single factor in the US judicial system.[6] Not surprisingly, therefore, the eyewitnessing literature abounds with examples of human fallibility and it is no coincidence that the British *Devlin Report* recommended that someone should not be convicted on the basis of eyewitness evidence alone. One reason for the unreliability of eyewitness evidence relates to the reconstructive nature of human memory. We saw in Bartlett's experiments (Chapter 2) that people use schemata to fill in gaps in their memories and this obviously happens in eyewitnessing too. The way questions are phrased, for example, can alter what people think they saw. In one famous experiment subjects saw a film of a car pile up. As part of the experiment some subjects were asked "How fast were the cars going when they *smashed into* each other?" and in the question put to others, *hit* was substituted for *smashed into*. Immediately afterwards subjects were asked how fast the cars were going, and those that heard the "smashed into" question estimated the speed to be higher than those who heard the "hit" question. A week later all the subjects were asked "Did you see any broken glass?"

Over twice as many of the subjects who had the "smashed into" question said there was broken glass compared with the "hit" question, even though no broken glass was there at all.[7] Presumably memory for the different verbs has called up different schemata about what could have happened, and this has influenced the reconstructive process.

Another well-known phenomenon is the **misinformation effect** in which, subsequent to viewing an event, subjects are given misleading information about that event. In one experiment, for example, subjects viewed an incident in which a man was using a hammer but then heard a narrative in which the instrument was described as a screwdriver. Subjects given the misinformation more readily agreed that the instrument was a screwdriver than those who did not.[8] One view of these studies is that the misinformation comes to "over-write" the old memory, effectively obliterating it and preventing accurate recall. An alternative view is that **demand characteristics** are at work in that people go along with the false suggestions even though they know they are inaccurate.[9] However, misinformation effects can be obtained even when a warning about the falsity of information is given. This suggests that demand characteristics cannot always explain things and the accepted view is that misinformation effects arise from a multiplicity of factors.[10]

A major criticism of misinformation effects is that they almost exclusively show that people are vulnerable to misleading information about peripheral information in a sequence of events. Thus studies have misled subjects about the brand name of a drink can or the name of a magazine on a desk. One can argue that what is most important is an individual's memory for the main or central features of an event. When this has been taken into account a rather different picture emerges. In one experiment people viewed videotapes of industrial accidents and then completed a questionnaire about what they had seen. It was found that it was more difficult to alter people's memory for central events using misleading questions—and more recent studies have confirmed this.[11] A related finding is that individuals who were good at identifying a criminal showed poorer memory for peripheral information associated with the event—a particularly important finding in the light of evidence that jurors are more impressed by witnesses who show good recall of peripheral detail.[12]

Confirmation bias is another phenomenon in which variations in schemata might affect what people remember. Essentially this is where people's recollection of an event corresponds not to the truth but to what they think should have happened in a given situation. This might be trivial, i.e. which of two football teams committed more fouls in a match, or more serious such as the roles of people of different races in a violent confrontation.

A major problem in eyewitnessing is that the police will often try to get a description of a criminal from a witness. The value of this critically depends on the accuracy of the description. Verbal descriptions are poor and there is evidence that asking for a verbal description actually makes the probability of accurate identification less likely.[13] One solution to this has been the development of facial reconstruction techniques, such as *Photofit*, in which subjects assemble the face of the criminal from different component pieces. Unfortunately people are not very good at using these methods even when the face they are trying to construct is familiar or in front of them on the screen. Figure 7.1 illustrates this, showing four photofits of the Cambridge rapist alongside his actual picture.[14]

There are many other factors that influence eyewitness testimony and, in so doing, caution us against the value of witness evidence in a trial. Contrary to common sense, for example, the confidence of a witness bears no relation to the accuracy of his or her evidence.[15] Eyewitnesses tend to overestimate the duration of events. There is also the same vs different race effect in recognition, showing that people recognise members of their own race better than members of other races—this appears to be because different parts of the face are crucial for recognition in different races. Status of the interviewer is important, with high-status interviewers obtaining more information from witnesses than low-status interviewers. However, a downside of this is that misleading information introduced by high-status interviewers is also more likely to be incorporated into memory.[16]

Given all the problems with eyewitness evidence what can be done to improve the ability of a witness? In Chapter 2 we saw

Figure 7.1: Four photofit attempts at reconstructing the face of the Cambridge rapist and his actual face.

the importance of context as a cue to memory. It follows, therefore, that eyewitness memory might improve if the context of the crime is somehow reinstated. In an early French version of this idea the actual crime scene (see Figure 7.2) was revisited, but this is not practical in general. An alternative approach is the **cognitive interview** which involves a set of retrieval strategies:

- Recreate mentally the scene of the crime, including how you felt at the time.
- Report everything you can think of even if the information is partial.
- Recount the incident in a number of different orders.
- Report from different perspectives, i.e. how the interviewee saw things compared with other people present.

The cognitive interview was found to be a more effective means of eliciting accurate information from memory. Many studies have subsequently shown that the cognitive interview enhances eyewitness memory in a variety of circumstances.[17]

Another crucial issue in eyewitness research is the line-up procedure which is employed by police forces around the world. For a line-up to be fair it must be the case that a witness could not figure out which person was the suspect on any basis other than their memory for the crime. Research has shown, however, that biases often exist and these result in many false identifications. There are, however, a number of suggestions that can reduce line-up error: witnesses should be told that the witness might not be in the line-up; the witness should not stand out in any way (e.g. look dishevelled); the person administering the line-up should not know who the suspect is so as to avoid any coercion; and witnesses should be asked how certain they are about their decision.[18] Unfortunately these points are often ignored and there is also evidence that defence lawyers are often unaware of the various biases that can exist in line-up procedures.[19]

The issue of improving eyewitness memory raises an additional question: Do police officers, because of their experience, make more reliable witnesses? Intuitively one would think so. Police training teaches policemen how to assess crime situations

Figure 7.2: An early attempt by French police at using context to reinstate memory for a crime.

and the motivation of policemen to remember the circumstances of a crime should be much higher. The results of research, however, show overwhelmingly that policemen do not make better witnesses. One study asked policemen and civilians to report any crimes seen in a 20-minute video. There were no group differences and policemen were seen as less flexible, tending to look out for crimes of a particular sort. In an experiment comparing students and police recruits it was found that the latter remembered more about the clothing of would-be criminals but overall their accuracy was no better than the students. An exception to the general rule is a recent Swedish study showing better eyewitness performance by police officers.[20]

FALSE MEMORY

The fallibility of human memory takes on a new dimension when we consider the phenomenon of **false memory**. In the last few years there has been almost an epidemic outbreak of adults suddenly "recovering" memories of sexual abuse. In many instances these recovered memories have taken on bizarre dimensions with accusations that parents subjected their children to Satanic rituals and other kinds of occult behaviour. The issue for the impartial psychologist is whether this phenomenon can really be true. Are there really, according to some estimates, tens of thousands of people with suppressed memories of sexual abuse or is there some other explanation about what is going on?

Undoubtedly there is some other explanation. This is not to say that sexual abuse of children is not a frightening reality or that a few adults may genuinely have suppressed memories of abuse. It is the sheer scale of the phenomenon that leads us to query what is going on. Fortunately the alternative explanation appears quite clear and can be linked to a therapeutic movement in the USA in which therapists confronted with a disturbed client were encouraged to investigate childhood sexual abuse as the principal explanation: "You know, in my experience, a lot of people who are struggling with the same problems you are, have often had some really painful things happen to them as kids—maybe they were beaten or molested." "It is crucial . . . that clinicians ask about sexual abuse during therapy."[21]

Inspired by books such as *The Courage to Heal*,[22] these therapists believed that "memory work" was an essential way of helping clients come to terms with their apparent traumatic past. Thus even though the client might initially have no recollection of abuse, the therapist should dig around relentlessly, often using leading questions, until the individual confronts the possibility that abuse may have taken place. To facilitate this, therapists often made extensive use of **hypnosis** when interviewing their clients. Most of us have seen hypnotists at work on TV shows and, observing the antics of hypnotised people, it is not hard to believe that hypnosis exerts some special power over an individual. Therapists using hypnosis with apparently abused adults believe that hypnosis has some special power and may be able to unlock memories that are suppressed under normal conditions.[23] Unfortunately this assumption is simply wrong. There have now been many experiments which show that hypnosis does not enhance memory at all—all hypnosis does is increase the amount people apparently remember not the accuracy—it is all too easy to mislead a hypnotised person.[24]

Many therapists using hypnosis believe that the technique can be used to regress back as far as birth.[25] This may go some way towards explaining why studies of recovered memory of sexual abuse typically show that the age at which the apparent sexual abuse took place is younger than the accounts of people who fully remember being abused. More importantly, the reported age is often below 4 and has frequently been in the first year of life. This is a particularly important finding because of the phenomenon of **infantile amnesia**—the finding that we can remember very little about what happened to us before the age of 4. Although the phenomenon is sound there is no agreed explanation of infantile amnesia although the popular explanation is that, around the age of 4, memory starts to operate in a different way and that memories formed before that time are incompatible with the new way memory works (see Chapter 4). Notwithstanding this difficulty, there is no doubt that memories of sexual abuse relating to years 0 to 4 should be treated as highly suspicious and indicative that they have somehow been manufactured.

Other phenomena associated with hypnosis include regressing to past lives and becoming a different person—very often someone of historical significance. While one may readily accept that hypnosis is producing massive amounts of misleading and almost nonsensical information, one still has to explain how these phenomena come about. Why should a normal adult regress to the womb and start screaming like a newborn baby or believe that she is Florence Nightingale? The answer for many is that hypnosis is an extreme form of **compliance** in which the hypnotised person comes under the control of the hypnotist and agrees to do or say anything that is requested.[26] This may seem odd but there is plenty of evidence elsewhere that people will comply in situations far more damaging than the average hypnotic situation. In one famous study, for example, subjects delivered what they thought were lethal electric shocks to other subjects who were incapable of learning. The explanation given was that the experimental setting somehow absolved them from responsibility.[27] It is not unreasonable to suppose that the hypnotic setting has a similar effect, leading the person to abandon his or her own rationality and comply with the wishes of the interviewer.

Returning to false memory it is clear that therapists have used repeated probing and suggestive questioning to patients. We saw earlier that, without hynoptic intervention, adults can be made to believe that things happened when they did not. Thus, the addition of hypnosis with repeated probing and leading questions is highly likely to result in people coming to believe that they really did experience things that were actually only suggested.[28] It should be noted, however, that the absence of hypnosis in the generation of recovered memory does not enhance credibility, as there is evidence that any form of therapy that introduces the possibility of suppressed memories of abuse can lead to the apparent recovery of memories.[29]

An interesting insight into the origins of recovered memory of sexual abuse was provided by a recent survey of members of the British False Memory Society.[30] Among the facts to emerge was that 87% of the accusers were female and that 96% of these accusations were against the biological father. While it is accepted that female child sexual abuse is more common, the distribution found in this study of 242 cases seems rather extreme and, given other evidence, the preponderance of accusations against biological rather than step-fathers also seems to be an imbalance. Together these facts suggest that other influences are at work—most notably the fact that the concept of recovered memory seems to have been closely linked to women's issues in general. The high frequency of allegations against biological fathers may be a reflection of therapy which seeks to find these unpleasant experiences in the early stages of life.

If you are not convinced by the above arguments then there is one other piece of evidence that must surely undermine the false memory syndrome as a widespread phenomenon. As noted earlier, proponents of recovered memory believe the problem is widespread. From this it follows that if we take a population of young adults who, from other evidence (e.g. medical), are known to have been sexually abused, we should expect to find a proportion of them who do not remember the abuse and are thus potential candidates for recovery phenomena. A recent study[31] examined several cases purporting to show this, but found the evidence weak. In some cases confirmation of the recovered memories was lacking, and in others victims were simply afraid to admit what had happened to them.

In sum, my opinion of false memory, like most scientific psychologists, is that recovered memory of sexual abuse is, at best, a rare phenomenon. We must therefore seek other explanations: biased therapy, mixed with the power of hypnosis, has had a great deal to do with it but we must not underestimate other factors such as media attention to the issue which, in turn, is likely to have encouraged presentation of apparently recovered memories.

THE FALLIBILITY OF CHILDREN'S MEMORY

In the early 1990s a set of extraordinary events took place in the Orkney Islands. Large numbers of children were removed from their parents on the grounds that parents were involved in widescale Satanic rituals. Subsequently all these allegations were dismissed and the children were returned to their families. Given that we have seen that adults can be the victims of suggestive questioning, it is probably not surprising that the events in the Orkneys took place. There is a large literature showing that children are more susceptible to the effects of suggestion than adults, and that strong age effects exist, with younger children being more suggestible than older ones.[32]

There have been a number of investigations of the misinformation effect in children. In one study children viewed a video and were then read a summary of what happened in the video. The summary contained some statements which were not true and it was found that younger children more readily accepted these false suggestions than older children. In a study aiming for greater realism, children between 3 and 15 years of age were asked questions about a medical examination they had received a few days earlier. There were strong age effects with young children more likely to agree with misleading questions, including those that suggested abuse (e.g. Did the doctor kiss you?).[33]

It should be borne in mind, however, that children are not always vulnerable and that children's memory for salient personal events can often be reliable. One study investigated 5- and 7-year-old children in which half of each age group received a physical check-up whereas the other half did not. Age effects in accuracy of recall, using both open-ended questioning and prompted recall by means of anatomically detailed dolls, were only significant for those children who were not touched. Thus, for those whom genital contact took place there was no age-related change in accuracy.[34]

While it is clear that, under many experimental conditions, children are more suggestible than adults, can the mechanisms at play in these experiments really explain the bizarre happening in the Orkney Islands? Recent work suggests that this is not the case. During the 1980s there were a series of "daycare ritual abuse cases" in which pre-school children made repeated allegations of sexual abuse in Satanic and other bizarre scenarios. While some psychologists have given credibility to these allegations, the majority of psychologists have looked for an explanation based on examining the interviewing techniques that were used on the children.

A recent study focused on the McMartin pre-school case, in which several teachers were accused of ritually abusing hundreds of children over a 10-year period.[35] Although court proceedings lasted nearly 10 years no conviction ever took place. Much of the case revolved around tape-recorded interviews with the alleged victims and many of the jurors criticised these interviews as using leading and suggestive questioning. However, suggestivity, as revealed in studies of the misinformation effect, was not the only factor contributing to the false recollections of the children. The study has examined the video tapes in question, and a large number of other factors—other than straightforward suggestibility—have emerged as important in making children go along with bizarre claims.

Telling children that other people have already revealed the desired information will tend to make a child conform. Thus, in one interview a child was told that "every single kid" had talked to the interviewer and "What we found out was that there's a whole lot of yucky secrets from your old school". Positive praise for a desired answer can also lead a child to produce a false memory. In one instance, following a long series of suggestive questions a child agreed that a teacher had photographed an entire class naked. The interviewer then congratulated the child: "Can I pat you on the head . . . look at what a good help you can be." Negative statements were also used to encourage children to agree to false information. One child, who denied any wrong-doing by the McMartin teachers, was told: "Are you going to be stupid, or are you going to be smart and help us here?"

Another technique used by the interviewers was to re-ask a question if they did not receive the desired answer. There is good evidence that children will respond to repeat questioning of this kind by changing their story. A last resort used by the interviewers when a child resisted all other attempts to confirm allegations of abuse was to invite speculation. Thus, using puppets, children would be asked to act what might have happened if there had been abusive behaviour by the teachers.

The above provide appalling examples of interview technique[36] but there has also been considerable research into improving the accuracy of child witness interviews. In the stepwise procedure the child first recalls information about an event without any prompting from the interviewer. Once a series of events are established the interviewer then homes in on specific facts—thus the child is only questioned about things he or she remembers.[37] Above we saw the value of the cognitive interview with adults and this has also been explored with child witnesses. One study showed that the cognitive interview technique allowed children to recall more accurate information from a staged event than those subjected to a standard interview technique. This is a promising result but younger children may have some trouble with certain aspects of the technique. It is not until around 5 or 6, for example, that children understand what it means to take the perspective of another person.[38]

You will recall that the idea behind the cognitive interview technique is that it helps to reinstate the context in which an event was originally experienced. From this it follows that reinstating the actual context in which an event was experienced should also be advantageous. There are, however, few examples of this, but a recent Israeli study attempted much greater realism. Children between 4 and 13 who were known victims of sexual abuse returned to the actual scene of the abuse. The results showed that the victims recalled additional details in the original context and that the interviewers were able to make greater sense of the children's statements.[39]

THE CHILD AS A WITNESS

From what we considered in Chapter 3, and from the above, we might conclude that it is distinctly risky to use children as witnesses in legal proceedings. Indeed, until relatively recently, it was generally considered that children were unreliable and that their evidence should be treated as suspect. However, the fact we now know so much more about children's memory and other related aspects of their development enables more informed decisions to be made about the value of child evidence.

In evaluating the value of children as witnesses it is particularly important to ascertain whether they can differentiate truth from lies. Distinguishing truth from lies does take a developmental course, with younger children being less able to explain the difference between truth and lies.[40] However, a subsequent study showed that these "competence questions" were not good predictors of memory accuracy, i.e. being able to explain the difference was not generally associated with better memory for an event.[41] It is also a mistake to assume that younger children are also more likely to lie and, providing questioning is done appropriately, that young children are more likely to accept fantasy as truth.[42]

The prevailing view now is that, with appropriate care, even the evidence of a 4-year-old may be admissible in a trial. However, in accepting the evidence great care must be applied to analysing how that evidence was obtained. Additional considerations concern how a witness is dealt with in court. An American study, for example, showed that lawyers frequently employed complex questions which the children did not understand. One 4-year-old child, for example, was asked the question: "On the evening of January 3rd, you did, didn't you, visit your grandmother's sister's house and did you not see the defendant leave the house at 7.30, after which you stayed the night?" Instead, it has been suggested that younger witnesses should be allowed to give evidence in their own words rather than respond to questions all the time.[43] Stress is also an important factor in that children may be frightened by the general situation and, more specifically, by confrontation with someone who has harmed them physically and/or mentally. To this end it is now frequently the case that children give evidence on video so as to reduce their stress.

SUMMARY

- Flashbulb memories are apparently highly accurate memories of highly significant events. They can, however, be inaccurate despite their vividness.
- A vivid memory is not necessarily a true one.
- Eyewitness memory can be distorted by the way questions are asked.
- Incorrect information presented after an event can distort memory for that event.
- Misleading information is more likely to affect peripheral detail rather than the central features of an event.
- Verbal descriptions and reconstructions of faces are poor.
- Eyewitness memory can be improved by means of the cognitive interview.
- Policemen do not, as a rule, perform more accurately as witnesses.
- False memory is the apparent recovery of memories relating to sexual abuse in early life.
- False memory appears to arise as a consequence of certain therapeutic methods.
- Hypnosis has been widely used in the "recovery" of memories of sexual abuse.
- The use of hypnosis as a means of enhancing memory is dubious because there is no evidence that it can help to recall information that is otherwise unavailable.
- Attempts to find people who are known, from other evidence, to have been sexually abused but do not remember have been unsuccessful.
- Children are more susceptible to the influences of misinformation and can, in certain circumstances, be led to believe that fantastic things have actually happened to them.
- Even very young children's memory for highly salient events can be good.
- To achieve high levels of false memory in children several questioning techniques have to be combined.

- Cognitive interview techniques can also enhance children's eyewitness memory.
- Children as young as 4 can be reliable witnesses but many factors have to be considered before accepting the evidence of children unreservedly.

NOTES AND REFERENCES

1. The original idea can be found in, Brown, R. & Kulik, J. (1982) Flashbulb memories. In U. Neisser (ed.) *Memory Observed: Remembering in Natural Contexts*, chap. 2. San Francisco: Freeman. A recent account of flashbulb memory is provided by Conway, M.A. (1995) *Flashbulb Memory*. Hove: Erlbaum.

2. Neisser's mistake: Neisser (1982) op. cit.[1] p. 45. Similar errors were also noted with regard to the *Challenger* disaster. Neisser, U. & Harsch, N. (1992) Phantom flashbulbs: False recollections of hearing the news about Challenger. In E. Winograd & U. Neisser (eds) *Affect and Accuracy in Recall*, pp. 9–31. Cambridge: Cambridge University Press. See also Conway, M.A. (1995) *Flashbulb Memories*. Hove, Sussex: LEA.

3. The case of John Demjanjuk is described by Loftus, E. & Ketcham, K. (1991) *Witness for the Defence: The Accused, the Eyewitness, and the Expert who Put Memory on Trial*. New York: St Martins Press. This book contains a number of true accounts concerning injustice based on faulty eyewitness evidence.

4. While it is received wisdom that memories formed during violent episodes are accurate, a recent study argues against this. Christainson, S.-A. & Huebinette, B. (1993) Hands up: A study of witnesses emotional reactions and memories associated with bank robberies. *Applied Cognitive Psychology*, 7, 365–379. This paper also reviews earlier evidence.

5. This account is taken from Baddeley, A.D. (1997) *Human Memory: Theory and Practice*, p. 18. Hove: Psychology Press.

6. Wells, G.L. (1993) What do we know about eyewitness identification? *American Psychologist*, **48**, 553–571. A much more extensive review of eyewitness research can be found in Ross, D.R. et al. (eds) (1994) *Adult Eyewitness Testimony: Current Trends and Developments.* New York: Cambridge University Press.

7. Loftus, E.F. & Palmer, J.C. (1974) Reconstruction of auto-mobile destruction: An example of the interaction between language and memory. *Journal of Verbal Learning and Verbal Behaviour*, **13**, 585–589.

8. An overview of these experiments is provided by Loftus, E.F. (1979) *Eyewitness Memory.* Cambridge. MA: Harvard University Press. See also Belli, R.F. & Loftus, E.F. (1996) The pliability of autobiographical memory: Misinformation and the false memory problem. In D.C. Rubin (ed.) *Remembering our Past: Studies in Autobiographical Memory.* New York: Cambridge University Press.

9. Zaragoza, M.S. & McCloskey, M. (1989) Misleading event information and the impaired memory hypothesis. *Journal of Experimental Psychology: General*, **118**, 92–99.

10. Lindsay, D.S. (1990) Misleading questions can impair eye-witnesses' ability to remember event details. *Journal of Experimental Psychology: Learning, Memory and Cognition*, **16**, 1077–1083.

11. Loftus (1979) op. cit.[8] See also Heath, W.P. & Erickson, J.R. (1998) Memory for central and peripheral actions and props after varied post-event presentation. *Legal and Criminological Psychology*, **3**, 321–346.

12. Wells, G.L. & Lieppe, M.R. (1981) How do triers of fact infer the accuracy of eyewitness identifications? Using memory for peripheral detail can be misleading. *Journal of Applied Psychology*, **66**, 682–687.

13. Dodson, C.S. et al. (1997) The verbal overshadowing effect: Why verbal descriptions impair face recognition.

14. From Baddeley (1997) op. cit.[5]

15. Luus, C.A.E. & Wells, G.L. (1994) Eyewitness identification confidence. In Ross et al. (1994) op. cit.[6]

16. Kassin, S.M. et al. (1989) The "general acceptance" of psychological research on eyewitness testimony. *American Psychologist*, **44**, 1089–1098.

17. The cognitive interview was developed by Geiselman, R.E. et al. (1985) Eyewitness enhancement in police interview: Cognitive retrieval mnemonics versus hypnosis. *Journal of Applied Psychology*, **70**, 401–412. Since then there has been extensive interest in this technique, see Fisher, R.P. (1995) Interviewing victims and witnesses of crimes. *Psychology, Public Policy and Law*, **1**, 732–764. Also, it appears that older people benefit more from cognitive interviewing: Mello, E.W. & Fisher, R.P. (1996) Enhancing older eyewitness memory with the cognitive interview. *Applied Cognitive Psychology*, **10**, 403–417.

18. Several chapters in Ross et al. (1994) op. cit.[6] discuss the issue of producing fair line-ups. See also, Wells, G.L. & Seelau, E.P. (1996) Eyewitness identification: Psychological research and legal policy on lineups. *Psychology, Public Policy and Law*, **1**, 765–791.

19. Stinson, V. et al. (1996) How effective is the presence of counsel safeguard? Attorney perceptions of suggestiveness, fairness, and correctability of biased lineup procedures. *Journal of Applied Psychology*, **81**, 64–75.

20. The Swedish study proving the exception is Christianson, S.-A. et al. (1988) Police personnel as eyewitnesses to a violent crime. *Legal and Criminological Psychology*, **3**, 59–72. This paper also reviews studies showing that police are no better at eyewitnessing than the general public.

21. There is now a vast literature on the false memory phenomenon. A good place to start is the two books which forcibly made the case that false memories are manufactured by therapists: Loftus, E.F. & Ketcham, K. (1994) *The Myth of Repressed Memory: False Memories and Allegations of Sexual Abuse*. New York: St. Martin's Press. Ofshe, R. & Watters, E. (1995) *Making Monsters: False Memories, Psychotherapy and Sexual Hysteria*. London: Deutsch. A recent edited book provides a variety of views on the issue: Conway, M.A. (1997) *Recovered Memories and False Memories*. Oxford: Oxford University Press. See also, Lindsay, D.S. & Briere, J. (1997) The controversy regarding recovered memories of childhood sexual abuse: Pitfalls, bridges and future dir-

ections. *Journal of Interpersonal Violence*, **12**, 631–647. Memon, A. & Young, M. (1996) Desperately seeking evidence: The recovered memory debate. *Legal and Criminological Psychology*, **2**, 131–154. An interesting article containing diametrically opposed views concerning false memory is Bass, E., Davis, L. & Coleman, L. (1997) Are memories of sex abuse always real? In S. Nolen-Hoeksema et al. (eds) *Clashing Views on Abnormal Psychology: A Taking Sides Custom Reader.* Guildford, CT: Dushkin/McGraw-Hill. There have been two UK working parties on the issue of false memory. The first—British Psychological Society (1995) *Recovered Memories: The Report of the Working Party of the British Psychological Society,* Leicester: The British Psychological Society—has been the subject of considerable criticism for its imprecision (see correspondence in *The Psychologist*, **11**, pp 465–467). A second report, by the Royal College of Psychiatrists has been much more decisive, concluding that there is a high probability that recovered memories of sexual abuse are false: Brandon, S. et al. (1998) Recovered memories of childhood sexual abuse. *British Journal of Psychiatry*, **172**, 296–307.

22. Bass, E. et al. (1988) *The Courage to Heal: A Guide for Women Survivors of Child Sexual Abuse.* New York: Harper & Row.

23. Yapko, M.D. (1994) Suggestibility and suppressed memories of abuse: A survey of psychotherapists' beliefs. *American Journal of Clinical Hypnosis*, **36**, 375–380.

24. See Dinges, D.F. et al. (1992) Evaluating hypnotic memory enhancement (hypermnesia and reminiscence) using multi-trial forced recall. Lynn, S.J. et al. (1997) Recalling the unre-callable: Should hypnosis be used to recover memories in psychotherapy? *Current Directions in Psychological Science,* **6**, 79–83.

25. Yapko (1994) op. cit.[23]

26. Wagstaff, G.F. (1981) *Hypnosis, Compliance and Belief.* Brighton: Harvester. Wagstaff has been the principal proponent of the compliance viewpoint. His view is that hypnotised subjects are simply role playing and, to back this up, he has conducted many experiments showing that ap-

parently "hypnotised" subjects will cease to be so if given a chance to own up. See, for example, Wagstaff, G.F. & Frost, R. (1996) Reversing and breaching posthypnotic amnesia and hypnotically created pseudomemories. *Contemporary Hypnosis*, **13**, 191–197.

27. Milgram. S. (1963) Behavioural study of obedience. *Journal of Abnormal and Social Psychology*, **67**, 371–378.

28. The susceptibility of people to change their minds when re-questioned about the same thing has led to the development of a psychological test which measures people's sensitivity to this manipulation: Gudjonsson, G. (1997) *The Gudjonsson Suggestibility Scales*. Hove: Psychology Press.

29. Brandon et al. (1998) op. cit.[21]

30. Gudjonsson, G. (1997) Accusations by adults of childhood sexual abuse: A survey of the members of the British False Memory Society (BFMS). *Applied Cognitive Psychology*, **11**, 3–18.

31. Pope, H.G. & Hudson, J.I. (1995) Can memories of childhood sexual abuse be repressed? *Psychological Medicine*, **25**, 121–126.

32. For a recent review see Qin, J. et al. (1997) Children's eyewitness testimony: Memory development in the legal context. In N. Cowan (ed.) *The Development of Memory in Childhood*. Hove: Psychology Press.

33. Ackil, J.K. & Zaragoza, M.S. (1995) Developmental differences in eyewitness suggestibility and memory for source. *Journal of Experimental Child Psychology*, **60**, 57–83.

34. Saywitz, K.J. et al. (1991) Children's memories of physical examinations involving genital touch: Implications for reports of child sexual abuse. *Journal of Consulting and Clinical Psychology*, **59**, 682–691.

35. Garven, S. et al. (1998) More than suggestion: The effect of interviewing techniques from the McMartin preschool case. *Journal of Applied Psychology*, **83**, 347–359.

36. For other examples of interviewing techniques that can tamper with children's memory, see Ceci, S.J. & Bruck, M. (1995) *Jeopardy in the Courtroom*. Washington, DC: American Psychological Association. Myers, J.E.B. et al. (1996)

Psychological research on children as witnesses: Practical implications for forensic interviews and courtroom testimony. *Pacific Law Journal*, **28**, 3–91.

37. Yuille, J.C. et al. (1993) Interviewing children in sexual abuse cases. In G.S. Goodman & B.L. Bottoms (eds) *Child Victims, Child Witnesses: Understanding and Improving Children's Testimony*, pp. 95–115. New York: Guilford.

38. See Qin et al. (1997) op. cit.[32] for an overview of these studies. See also, McCauley, M.R. & Fisher, R.P. (1996) Enhancing children's eyewitness testimony with the cognitive interview. *Psychology, Law and Criminal Justice. International Reviews in Research and Practice*, pp. 127–134. Berlin: De Gruyter.

39. Hershkowitz, I. et al. (1998) Visiting the scene of the crime: Effects on children's recall of alleged abuse. *Legal and Criminological Psychology*, **3**, 195–207.

40. Pipe, M.-E. & Wilson, J.C. (1994) Cues and secrets: The influences of children's event reports. *Developmental Psychology*, **30**, 515–525.

41. Goodman, G.S. et al. (1991) Children's memory for stressful events. *Merrill-Palmer Quarterly*, **37**, 109–158.

42. Melton, G.B. (1981) Children's competence to testify. *Law and Human Behaviour*, **5**, 73–85.

43. Saywitz, K.J. et al. (1993) Credibility of child witnesses: The role of communicative competence. *Topics in Language Disorders*, **13**, 59–78.

INDEX

intentional learning 20
intrinsic context 24

James, William 3, 4, 6, 21

Korsakoff's syndrome 12, 70, 92, 93,
    111, 115, 119, 121

Law of Disuse 35
learning, early 43–5
Lewinski, Monica 53
line-up procedure 140
Loftus, Elizabeth 18, 19
Loftus, Geoffrey 18, 19
long-term store memory (LTS) 3, 4–7
    organisation of 7–9
lorazepam 98

magnetic resonance imaging (MRI)
    scan 65, 67, 77, 90, 103
malingering 76–8
mamillary bodies 12
marijuana 7, 26, 27, 97
memory battery 69–71
memory disorder, genuineness of
    76–8
memory indices 70
memory strategies 50, 126
mental imagery 126
metabolic dysfunction 65
metamemory 52, 123
method of loci 126
midazolam 98
misinformation effect 137–8
mnemonic aids 126
mood congruency theory 27
Morbus–Cushing syndrome 102
multi-infarct dementia (MID) 95
multiple personality (MP) 100
multiple sclerosis 85

Neisser, Ulric 135
neocortex 10
neurones 6, 55–7
neuropage 126
neuropsychological assessment 68–9
neuroradiological investigation 65
neurotransmitter 6
Nixon, Richard 22

normative data 70
novelty preference 43

object hiding 48
operant conditioning 44
organic memory disorder 99
organisation 50

panencephalopathies 95
Paris, Texas 99
Parkinson's disease 85
Penfield, Wilder 18
percentile ranks 71
permanent memory loss 85–95
Photofit 138, 139
Pick's disease 95
Polyanna effect 27
positron emission tomography (PET)
    65, 68, 77, 103
post-morbid period 74
post-traumatic amnesia (PTA) 88
post-traumatic stress disorder 101–3
preference judgements 119
pre-morbid period 74
primacy effect 5
primary memory 3, 6
priming 30, 119
proactive interference 36
probe-digit technique 4
procedural memory 7, 117–18
processing resources 51
processing speed hypothesis 56
psychoactive states 26
psychogenic loss of memory 98–103
psychogenic memory disorder 99
psychology of memory 3–4
psycho-sexual theory of
    development 49

recall 23, 53
recency effect 4, 98, 112
recognition 23
recognition memory 53
Recognition Memory Test (RMT) 72,
    78
recollection 23
reconstructive memory 20–3
recovered memory 100, 144–5
rehearsal 50

Index compiled by Annette Musker

Related titles of interest...

Mind Myths
Exploring Popular Assumptions About the Mind and Brain
Edited by SERGIO DELLA SALA
This book shows that science can be both entertaining and creative. It explores various 'mind myths' – neurological and cognitive phenomena which capture people's curiosity, for example: Can playing a patient's favourite music resuscitate them from a coma? Do humans really use only 10% of their brain? Can we learn whilst we are asleep? These and many more questions are answered, with full, scientifically reliable explanations given.
0471 983039   March 1999   310pp   Paperback

Handbook of the Psychology of Interviewing
Edited by AMINA MEMON and RAY BULL
This is an authoritative text on the psychology of interviewing - reviewing diagnosis and assessment in several contexts, including social, medical, forensic and occupational. It covers a wide range of interview techniques.
0471 974439   February 1999   380pp   Hardback

Handbook of Applied Cognition
Edited by FRANCIS T. DURSO
This text presents a wealth of expertise on the applications of cognitive psychology. It offers comprehensive coverage of the key areas, such as Business and Industry, Computers and Technology, Education and Information, and Health and Law.
0471 252034   April 1999   904pp   Hardback